Praise for Estelle Bi

'Estelle is an incredible lifelong friend, mentor and heart whisperer. She's always been an extraordinary inspiration for me with her boundless wisdom and healing energy. Estelle is our best kept secret and now the world gets to meet her. Get ready to manifest your True Essence and live the life of your dreams. This book is about to change some lives.'
CHARLOTTE TILBURY MBE

'*Manifest Your True Essence* is a profound exploration of the transformative power of the heart. With wisdom rooted in both ancient traditions and modern science, Estelle guides readers on a journey to clear blocks, embrace their truth and manifest their highest potential.'
DEEPAK CHOPRA

'This book will open your eyes, touch your heart and change your life forever. Within these pages, Estelle draws from her years of wisdom and experience to create a powerful framework for true healing.'
FEARNE COTTON

'Estelle Bingham reaches the parts that others cannot reach. A heart whisperer and energetic healer, she is part wise woman, part cosmic force. The sheer power of her alchemy is not to be underestimated, if you are prepared to suspend some disbelief and activate some faith. This is a new way to tread an ancient path. Manifestation is deeply fashionable, but this is where manifestation meets love and divine energy.'
ANNABEL RIVKIN, *ES* MAGAZINE

'Connecting with your True Essence is the only way to experience a genuine, authentically fulfilling and meaningful life. This book will show you the way. It's a pure treasure you will absolutely love.'
SONIA CHOQUETTE, BESTSELLING AUTHOR OF *ASK YOUR GUIDES*

'*Manifest Your True Essence* is a powerful and profound guide to rediscovering your inner self and navigating a life of purpose, meaning and fulfilment. With practical tools and deep insights, it empowers you to heal, evolve and live in alignment with your highest and true potential. Prepare for a transformative journey that nurtures resilience, cultivates self-trust and inspires lasting change. A must read.'

ANITA MOORJANI, *NEW YORK TIMES* BESTSELLING AUTHOR OF *DYING TO BE ME*

'Wow! *Manifest Your True Essence* is a powerful and important read. Estelle has managed to interweave spiritual, scientific and practical wisdom to create a guidebook to true healing. Her words feel like mystic poetry and medicine for the soul – wise, heartfelt and transformational. A must read for anyone feeling stuck in any area of their life. Thank you for this brilliant book.'

MAUDE HIRST, ACTOR AND AUTHOR OF *INTUITIVE WHISPERS ORACLE*

'There's only one word for Estelle Bingham's practice: transformative. Or maybe two: utterly transformative.'

GOOP

'My life has been utterly transformed by Estelle and the heart-led healing and spirituality she so luminously embodies and shares so powerfully in love and light with the world. As a scientist, my sceptical and avoidant heart has been irrevocably broken open by Estelle and my soul awakened and transformed. This book should be read by all who seek love, purpose and connection.'

GAILLE MACKINNON, BA, MSc, MCSFS, MCIfA, FRAI (ChFA), CONSULTANT FORENSIC ANTHROPOLOGIST

'When you are running on zero, feeling physically, mentally and emotionally defeated, Estelle Bingham is the healer to get you out of your funk and restore your hope.'

TATLER

'Bingham is the rock 'n' roll cool girl of the healing world. She has the crystals, Zen insight and ability to make those who spend time with her feel there's more promise and purpose in their life than when they arrived.'

'Modern-age healer'

'The real charm... is the hands-on healing from Estelle Bingham, whose holistic crystal therapy has the beauty crowd beguiled.'

'Body & Soul, established in 1996, is a revolutionary UK trauma charity dedicated to liberating children, young people and families from the devastating, limiting and life-shortening effects of childhood adversity. We are deeply thankful for all Estelle has brought to Body & Soul. I know wholeheartedly that Body & Soul and many individuals who are part of the community would not be who we were meant to be without Estelle's nourishment, love and bravery.'

Manifest Your
True Essence

Clear Your Blocks, Find Your Joy, Live Your Truth

ESTELLE BINGHAM

Founder of the True Essence Process™

HAY HOUSE

Carlsbad, California • New York City
London • Sydney • New Delhi

Published in the United States by: Hay House LLC, www.hayhouse.com® • P.O. Box 5100, Carlsbad, CA, 92018-5100

Text © Estelle Bingham, 2025

Illustrations © Lizzie Clark (www.lizzieclark.com), 2025

The moral rights of the author have been asserted.

The information given in this book should not be treated as a substitute for professional medical advice; always consult a medical practitioner. Any use of information in this book is at the reader's discretion and risk. Neither the author nor the publisher can be held responsible for any loss, claim or damage arising out of the use, or misuse, of the suggestions made, the failure to take medical advice or for any material on third-party websites.

A catalogue record for this book is available from the British Library.

Tradepaper ISBN: 978-1-4019-7582-1
E-book ISBN: 978-1-83782-056-6
Audiobook ISBN: 978-1-83782-055-9

10 9 8 7 6 5 4 3 2 1

Printed in the United States of America

This product uses responsibly sourced papers, including recycled materials and materials from other controlled sources.

The authorized representative in the EU for product safety and compliance is Penguin Random House Ireland, Morrison Chambers, 32 Nassau Street, Dublin D02 YH68, Ireland. https://eu-contact.penguin.ie

The greatest mystery will only be revealed
to you through the heart.

This is the journey we must take to return to wholeness.

Contents

Introduction

When clients arrive on my doorstep – all ages, walks of life, races and religions, believers, non-believers, sceptical, doubtful, fearful, curious and everything in between – they have usually been ushered or prompted by either their higher-self soul energy or their guides, and they aren't even fully conscious that this sort of energy exists. They just know something isn't quite right, or they're at a crossroads, in the deep trenches of a crisis, or feeling stuck, or lost, and have nowhere else to turn. I'm often the last-chance saloon.

Invariably, when they have settled into my therapy room, a palpable sense of panic will begin to fill the space between us.

Ten minutes early, I wait outside Estelle's house. It's taken three months to get this appointment, so there's already a sense of anticipation building up inside me. I glance at the green door, then rub my palms on the lemon balm sprawling from the front garden.

Eventually, Estelle pops her head out of the top window, assuring me I'm in the right place. I'm taken aback by her warmth. There's a childlike cheek to her expression that I wasn't expecting. I'm not entirely sure what I was expecting, but it wasn't this.

Her previous client ushers me up the steep white staircase. Suddenly my stomach ties itself in knots and my usual cocky bravado leaves the house and goes down the street along with the former client. My hands shake as I untie my boots.

Meaningless words stream from my mouth as I try to appear poised. I fail miserably.

Estelle ushers me into a candlelit room and proceeds to plonk giant crystals on various parts of my body. Their weight pushes me down into the fabric of her sofa.

'Breathe deeply,' she soothingly instructs, clocking the uncertainty etched across my brow.

There's a dense atmosphere in this room. You could cut it with a knife. It's powerful, charged with a femininity and an almost ancestral quality. I panic, wondering what the hell I've signed up for.

Estelle sits, cloaked in melancholy... my melancholy. After a pregnant pause, she burrows through the thick air between us and latches onto my gaze. I instantly feel stripped naked. Seen.

Kit Sinclair

Our greatest fear is that if we are fully seen, if we drop the armour and stand there – in the stark rawness of authentic vulnerability – then the parts of ourselves that we have suppressed, muted and relegated to the shadows will be *judged* by others – in the way that we so harshly judge ourselves.

•••

I want you to know there is life beyond the fear of being exposed, beyond the old hurts and shame that tell you it's too dangerous to risk being fully seen, even though it's what you truly wish for. You may have to shed a few skins to get there, and shine a light into some dark corners to find the way, but the place beyond is a heart space that births miracles and generates a frequency of grace, flow, healing and belonging. It will help you choose wisely and bring you what you need. You will remember your passion and discover your purpose. You will tend to your inner fire, anchor into a deep truth about who you are and manifest your intuition and your unique gifts – your True Essence.

When we are out of touch with our True Essence, we are like a ship without a North Star or compass. We are unable to ever truly plot a navigable course to a safe harbour or master the turbulent tides of our lives. Our inner GPS system is officially kaput!

This lifetime is about building a safe harbour for ourselves – a 'safe place' within, where we can come home to ourselves. No one can do that for us. But through the process that I will present here, you will learn how to do it for yourself.

The foundations of this safe place will be built on a deeper understanding of the multi-dimensional reality of love and your ship will drop anchor there through the power of your heart.

Your sense of self will no longer rely on other people's approval, ideas or opinions of you. Those days of desperately seeking external validation are coming to an end now. You will find your voice, harness the courage to speak your truth and maintain healthy boundaries that support your new way of being in the world.

Possibility, empowerment and hope are woven through each of the chapters in this book, and my wish is that once you have completed it, not only will you have a strong, easy-to-access practice that will support your True Essence, but you will have begun to deepen your relationship with the magic, power and beauty of your heart and your cosmic blueprint. This process will also help you develop your connection to the quantum field, an energetic frequency that can expedite your ability to heal, manifest and cultivate a sense of mastery in your life.

•••

The Holy Grail of healing is transformation. Not fleeting transformation, but grounded, life-changing, karma-clearing transformation – tangible shifts that gather momentum and create daily miracles that we can touch, feel and experience at the very core of our being.

Over the past 20 years I have helped thousands of people heal their trauma and transform their lives from the inside out. Every morning I prepare my space and pray. I ask that all the souls I have the privilege of meeting that day will touch their divinity, and I know we are meant to meet, because everything is always as it is meant to be.

I have also prayed for this moment: that I would write a book and it would find its way to whoever needed it. You are meant to be reading these words at this time; somehow, we have both chosen to meet in this way. I am setting the intention that these chapters are a companion and support on your journey back to your True Essence and a life where you express your truth and embody your authentic joy and potential.

Our True Essence is our infinite nature, the part of us that never dies, and when we have connected with it, our guidance and intuition are strong. When this channel isn't cluttered with the chit-chat of internal negative self-talk and beliefs, or the endless lists of stuff that our ego and toxic fear love to tirelessly remind us about, we are able to create space in our consciousness to grow and evolve. We are free to commune with nature, our ancestors, our family in the light and the Divine every day. We have the power to co-create our reality. That is what this book is about.

These chapters are a distillation of the many hours I have spent bearing witness to the preciousness of what makes us human – the trials and tribulations of what Buddhists call *samsara*, this earthly dimension of pain and suffering. It is everything we already know, but need to be reminded of.

The practices are pretty simple. They include slight adjustments to the way you show up every day to bring you into alignment.

You don't need to feel overwhelmed. Take your time to pause and reread sections. Start a new journal, make notes and, above all, remember to have compassion for yourself. You have actually got this!

Let's make some *magic*.

PART I

Softening

'Although the road is never-ending,
take a step and keep walking.
Do not look fearfully into the distance...
on this path let the Heart be your Guide.'

RUMI

CHAPTER 1

The Golden Seed

'The privilege of a lifetime is to become who you truly are.'
CARL JUNG

When I began writing this book, I sat down at my computer with the very clear intention that it would change lives. I didn't want it to be another 'self-help' book that would gather dust, half-read, on a pile of other self-help books on a bedside table or an obscure shelf. I wanted to refine what I had learned on a deep level over the two decades since I began dedicating my life to being of service to Spirit to bring you something practical, tangible and truly empowering. These chapters serve as a living, breathing process that will work in the same way as if we were actually together in a room over a series of sessions. This is the True Essence Process.

When I had my first very clear out-of-body experience at 22, in the middle of the day, lying on a sofa in Chelsea, London, among other things I saw an incredible light web matrix surrounding the planet and felt the presence of Christ. I was also told in no uncertain terms that there was *no space* and *no time*. Thirty years later, quantum mechanics backs up that message. So, let us begin from that premise. We may not be meeting in physical form, but as you read these words, we are meeting in an energetic inter-dimensional place. And my sincere intention is that as you begin to integrate the practices of this book into your everyday life, you will meet the miraculous beauty of your mystic, spiritual heart and manifest everything that this lifetime has in store for you.

'The Spiritual Heart is formless and limitless.
It is our connection with the Divine –
like an inner sun.
We are not awakening the heart –
we are reawakening our memory of it.'
SRI RAMA KRISHNA

Intention

Intention is everything. It sets energy into motion, which means it seeds reality. You may already be familiar with the spiritual and scientific truth that energy follows thought. This is a basic universal law that has been understood in certain circles for millennia, but has been circulating in the mainstream for over 20 years now as the Law of Attraction, and more recently as the power of manifestation.

In its simplest form, the Law of Attraction is about vibration, or frequency. It's the law of 'like attracts like'. So, positive thoughts and emotions, which are high-vibrational and transmit a positive frequency into the world, will attract things, people and experiences that are a vibrational match into your life. And the same is true for negative thoughts and emotions. They are low-vibrational and will attract the corresponding energy into your field. If you're stuck in the revolving door of a negative mindset, or surrounded by people who aren't good for you, by default you will manifest more of the same.

'Everything is energy and that's all there is to it.
Match the frequency of the reality you want and you
cannot help but get that reality. It can be no other way.'
ALBERT EINSTEIN

Imagine standing at your bedroom window. You are broadcasting your own personal radio show to the world. You are the transmitter and the radio waves are emanating from inside you.

Whatever it is that we focus our attention on will eventually take shape around us. Which is why we all have the power to change our lives, right? Well, yes *and* no...

Yes, it's true that if we raise our vibration, good things will undoubtedly begin to manifest in our lives. But there's definitely a ceiling to what the universe can deliver to us if our unconscious thoughts don't tally with our conscious ones. People tell me all the time how they've been obsessively focusing on manifesting, making vision boards and repeating affirmations, but nothing seems to change for them. This is my response: 'You can repeat those affirmations till the cows come home, but if you haven't started the work of reprogramming your unconscious mind, you haven't got a hope in hell of ever reaping the rewards of all your hours of amazing effort and dedication.' Period.

This is because when we carry energetic blocks in our unconscious, the messages that we are transmitting to the universe are distorted, undecipherable and phenomenally powerful. As neuroscience now confirms, only 5 per cent of our brain activity is actually conscious; the other 95 per cent is unconscious. So, it's only when we commit to exploring and transmuting the blocks in our unconscious that we can unlock our 'access all areas' code. This code brings us into direct contact with our True Essence and the quantum field, where everything is possible.

Let me take you into a secret garden. Read this visualization to the end and then close your eyes and walk yourself gently through the steps again. Jot down the images that emerge for you in your journal at the end. Don't overthink it. Allow the images to form effortlessly in your mind.

Find a path and take a few steps along it, then come to a gate or a wooden door. Take a deep breath and open it. Step into a garden – *your* garden.

This is a place that represents how your life looks and feels right now. What time of year is it? Is the garden shadowy or bathed in full or dappled sunlight? Is it overgrown and full of thorns? Can you see trees, flowers or grass? What is living in your garden? Are there dragonflies, butterflies, bees and birds, or is it silent and empty of life? Does it feel welcoming or spooky? Trust whatever images pop into your mind.

It's our job, together, to turn this garden into a place of serenity and beauty. We'll trim the shrubs and dig up the weeds. We'll also plant a golden seed. This will be a seed that carries the vision of your limitless future. You'll get to plant it wherever you like, because this is your sacred space.

For that precious seed to flourish, you'll have to sow it in fertile soil. The soil in this garden represents your unconscious mind.

To manifest your True Essence, you need to clear your unconscious mind of blocks and nourish it with love and care. This will create the truly fertile ground for your golden seed to take root and grow into a beautiful future.

The way to this future is through the heart. When we activate our heart energy, we evolve and heal in the quantum field, which leads to exponential personal growth. This is where we can alchemize the blocks and beliefs that are holding us back with a precision and wisdom that is not known by the mind.

You may have explored some of the themes in this process within other therapeutic settings. The difference here is that you're accessing and engaging the three chambers of the heart, which means you'll embody the shifts you make in a very different way. You'll feel the transformation in your bones.

First, we bring awareness to the physical heart, which is essentially your heartbeat and breath. Then we spend time with the emotional heart, which is like a storeroom of unprocessed emotion, or a library that tenderly holds every aspect and detail of your story, even the chapters your conscious mind may have forgotten. From here we're able to access the mystic heart, which is essentially home to your soul and dwells at the core of your being. Your mystic heart is the gateway to peace, unconditional love, self-acceptance and a truly authentic life. It will also become your anchor, steadying you on the ever-changing sea of life.

The reality is there are times when we wake to sunshine and blue skies and other times when storm clouds are gathering on the horizon. Life will continually ebb and flow. There will always be days that feel better than others. But when we have anchored into our mystic heart, we are no longer at the mercy of that energy. We cultivate healthy resilience and no longer spiral downwards into negative reactions, loops or old patterns.

'Those who are truly wise will remain unmoved by feelings of happiness and suffering, fame and disgrace, praise and blame, gain and loss. They will remain calm like the eye of a hurricane.'
BUDDHA

For now, let's return to the notion of intention. There isn't a better place to start. When we get super-clear about our intention, the universe responds with a big smile. Magic happens. So, let's kick off this adventure as we mean to go on.

My intention is that within these pages you will find a safe place to feel all of the feelings that your emotional heart has been holding for you since your birth, so that you can access the wisdom of your mystic heart. As the walls that surround your heart gently soften and melt, your ability to trust its guidance will grow. Your heart's wisdom will become known to you, and over time you will find yourself amazed by its vastness – an ocean of infinite length, breadth and depth, a place of great beauty buried deep within you. You will know something of the true face of Love. And from this place, you will manifest your True Essence.

Now I invite you to think about *your* intention, and write it down. So, grab your journal and a pen and settle into your space. Write down:

~ three things you intend to transform and release through this process and...

~ three things you intend to manifest in your life through this work.

We are co-creating an alchemical container of endless possibility together and your active participation lets the universe know that you've arrived at the station and are ready to board the train! Even if you feel that your deepest desires are completely out of reach right now, just showing up on the platform is enough to get the train headed down the track.

This is the moment when you can begin to thread the invisible power of magic, an energy that surrounds us in the unseen world, through the eye of your needle of possibility.

Make it part of your practice to come back and reread your intentions as you begin each new chapter of this book. Feel free to add sentences, words and new visions to your original intentions as they emerge for you.

There are many spiritual, shamanic, religious, non-dual paths and modern wellness practices out there that can get the ball rolling. In the end, all paths lead to the same place: back to the feet of Love. So, there's nothing new in this book. It's a well-trodden route. I'm just bringing you a process that I was guided to by Spirit and that, in my experience, works.

Like you, I have left a dimension of pure divine love and light and I'm here on the Earth plane to resolve karma with people and places, fulfil sacred contracts, complete life purposes, and start, resume and finish levels of what I like to call 'soul school'. And, like you, I'm on my way back home.

> 'Our birth is but a sleep and a forgetting;
> the Soul that rises with us, our life's Star,
> hath had elsewhere its setting
> and cometh from afar;
> not in entire forgetfulness
> and not in utter nakedness,
> but trailing clouds of glory do we come
> from God, who is our home.'
> WILLIAM WORDSWORTH

When you thread the invisible
power of magic through the eye
of your needle of possibility, you're
weaving the strands of your current
life into a new vision of your future.

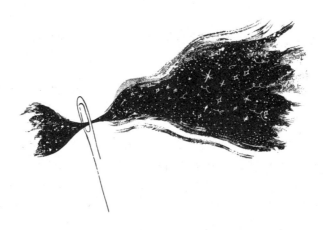

Most of us feel a longing to go back home. Like a door banging on its frame in the wind, there is always something niggling at the back of our mind, telling us that we're out of kilter. Alone. Possibly lonely. Feeling unloved. What we're longing for is to return to Love.

Without love, life is rendered life-less. We may be unconscious of how deeply a lack of love impacts our reality, but at a cellular level it's truly cavernous – a hollow echo resounds in the depths of our being when there is separation from this profound energy.

When we are living a heart-centred life, on the other hand, we learn how to love ourselves enough to be at one with ourselves. When our self-love increases, we feel the energy of universal connection more in our lives. Then slowly we learn how to be at one with all things.

In a sense, we are already there.

Universal Connection

Science has established that all things, be they gas, liquid or solid, are composed of infinitesimal specks called atoms. These form the building blocks of the world we see around us.

Science has also established that each atom has a centre, a nucleus, where there is an electrical current that forces even smaller particles – electrons, neutrons and protons – to whizz around one another very quickly.

So, scientists have finally proved what prophets, shamans, mystics and spiritual teachers have known for thousands of years: that at the centre of *all* things is *energy* and that we are *all* connected on an energetic level. But we've lost touch with this universal truth.

Evolution shows us that we're at the top of the 'food chain', and since the advent of the West's domination and control of the natural world, we have blown this privilege completely out of proportion. *En masse* it appears that we've bought into the idea that we're the most intelligent life on Earth!

Yes, it's true that we've built great cities and palaces and travelled into space and down to the darkest reaches of the ocean. Our achievements are a profound testament to our collective endeavours and ingenuity.

But lest we forget, without the trees, the plants and the natural world around us, we would be unable to breathe. We would cease to exist.

Today, we find ourselves in a culture where we have mostly disregarded or forgotten this *universal connection*. So, how intelligent are we really?

We may have forgotten it, but we are still custodians of the Earth's energy, and part of it. We are all made of the same stuff – connected, *interconnected*. And yet so many of us are not only disconnected from the world around us, but from our own being too.

I walked into Estelle's office thinking I wanted guidance on what my career path should be – corporate law, the life I'd had for eight years, or a wine business I'd recently started with my fiancé. What I realized within minutes of meeting Estelle was that my hesitation in life had very little to do with my career – far from it.

On that first visit I lay down, surrounded by crystals (having never touched a crystal in my life), and was engulfed by the realization that I was completely unrooted. I had absolutely no idea who I was – person, being, soul, woman, zero! This realization didn't come from asking the age-old question 'Who am I?', but from a heart-led meditation that Estelle guided me through.

In that meditation, I met myself for the very first time. There I was, an old soul who had patiently waited for a connection for the last 31 years.

Elisha

I'm here to tell you that it's never too late to make that connection with yourself. It's never too late to start *loving* – to start *loving* yourself, to start *loving* your life. It's never too late to *invite love* into your life. To experience what it truly means to *love* and *be loved* in your entirety.

You deserve to manifest abundance, success and kind, loving and authentic relationships in all areas of your life. You deserve to look in the mirror and really love all that you see. To access the *oceans of infinite love* that surround you in the unseen world and, through your earthly relationships, connect back to Source and to the whole.

To do this, you need to open your heart...

CHAPTER 2

Opening the Heart

'The way is not in the sky; the way is in the heart.'
BUDDHA

So many people arrive at their first session with me demoralized, worn down, at breaking point, many miles from home, their inner sanctuary. They are mostly white-knuckling around their negative self-talk and beliefs. This is a visual that Spirit shows me when a person is frozen in a state of self-loathing.

We can say the most hurtful things to ourselves about our mind, body and spirit all day long. Our negative self-talk can be so deeply ingrained that it actually goes unnoticed. We merge with the internal abuse and it just becomes the lens through which we view the world. Or we may experience the negative self-talker or inner critic as an obsessive, intrusive, all-consuming voice that we're actively battling to overcome every day. But that negative self-talk inserts itself everywhere, especially when we might get to experience a little bit of joy or feel worthy or proud of ourselves. Our destructive dialogue is constantly telling us that we're everything from completely unlovable to the worst type of imposter. There isn't an insult that's off-limits!

I'm here to tell you that when you open your heart and activate your heart space, this noise will quieten down. Seriously. I asked some of my students and clients how connecting with their heart energy had impacted their lives...

'Since connecting with my heart... shifts are actually happening in my life. It feels like healing on steroids.'

ANNISA

'I am finding I can return to a feeling of calm and peace. It's like a light that doesn't blow out. Opening my heart has helped me live life to my full potential, find joy, grow, laugh and feel the best I can.'

GRANIA

'Everything that I knew in my head about the energy of love, I actually feel in my heart. It has been a phenomenal and revolutionary experience.'

ADRIANNA

'Connecting to my heart has helped me connect to my intuition, my truth and my soul. I understand the intelligence of my body, especially when it's trying to tell me things my mind doesn't understand yet. I operate less from my ego and am not worried about what people will think of me. I feel so much less alone in the world, and knowing my heart has such intelligence, wisdom and power gives me the most incredible guiding system to lead me in love for the rest of my life.'

ABBY

'I have discovered my inner self and a deep love for myself.'

JINDER

*'I no longer feel the need to control my surroundings, to force my
life in a certain direction. Instead, I connect with my heart, follow
my intuition and I trust. This may sound like a small thing, but living
life in this way on a daily basis has been such a huge release for
me, and as a result life flows and I enjoy it so much more.'*

EMMA

*'It's been a game-changer. This heart-led work has given me a
reference point for the feeling of love that I never had before, a sense
of myself that had eluded me. I feel like I've finally come home.'*

ANNA

*'Connecting to my now-activated heart has brought me extraordinary
love and deep connection. It's like I have woken from a very
deep sleep and I'm seeing and feeling for the very first time.'*

GAILLE

The heart is so much more than a mechanical pump, but we've forgotten it.
Our time together now is about remembering and about allowing the alchemy
of the heart to work its magic and reconnect us to Love and our True Essence.

The Journey to Love

*'Hello? Heart to Earth: Do we have a signal?
I repeat: Heart to Earth... is there life in there?
This is your mission, should you agree to it: Journey back to Love.'*

As you open your heart, you will feel a growing sense of connection to
yourself, nature and the universe. Synchronicities will start to happen, signs will

appear and different relationships and new opportunities will begin to show up in your life.

Set your own pace as you start this process. Be kind to yourself. We are all perfectly imperfect and the healing journey is messy, and never, ever linear, so take your time. The road can get dark sometimes and feel as if it will never end. But know this: our breakdowns are actually *breakthroughs* in disguise.

The Sufi teacher, philosopher and poet Rumi wrote, 'The wound is the place where the light enters you.' He lived in the 13th century, but those words are as relevant today as they were back then. When we face our pain and allow our feelings to crack us wide open, we allow the light in for a new day to begin. Alchemizing our wounds, turning pain into opportunity, connects us to our fierce grace and courage.

So, however imperfect you might feel right now, you're on your way. You've got this. And I'll be with you every step of the way.

• • •

I've been on a messy journey myself. I have distinct memories of some of my very first moments in this dimension, three snippets that happened in close succession. The first is of being in a large room of what I would later understand was a maternity hospital, with the hazy outline of a floor-length window in the foreground. The second is of hovering just above my baby body, and the third is of being handed to my father, with his younger sister, my Auntie Kathleen, standing by his side.

What I didn't know then was that I had dropped into an incarnation with profoundly active mother and father wounds on both the female and male sides. The alchemizing of this wound has informed the direction of my lifetime so far. It is at the core of my purpose and has gifted me with more wisdom and illumination than I could possibly have imagined when, having dragged myself, depressed and lost, through university, I woke up one morning utterly engulfed by my childhood trauma. This was a dark night of the soul.

When I read my journals from that time, I realize that my suffering came from a very old, suppressed sense of abandonment and isolation that had resurfaced with a vengeance. I was consumed by the feeling that no one ever had my back and that I would never be truly understood. It was little me against the world, and I got to the point where I didn't want to live any more.

My thoughts circled around two distinct themes: betrayal, disappointment and absence in the masculine, and heartbreak and rejection in the feminine. My father just hadn't been present enough for me growing up. I felt that I had been 'left' by him, abandoned. This pattern had been repeated by my mother's long-term boyfriend and, not unsurprisingly, I had unconsciously manifested emotionally unavailable partners in my two significant relationships up to that point. My shattered experience of the feminine, a result of the fractured relationship I had with my mother, had left me with a deep terror of being vulnerable and intimate...

And on top of all of that, I was a classic toxic empath – an empath without any boundaries. So, all of my friends would come to me with their problems, but it wouldn't ever enter their minds that I might need to go to them with mine. The strong, capable mask that I presented to the world was convincing. It wasn't that I wasn't emotional and open with my friends; I was, but more often than not I ended up 'rescuing' everyone around me. I believed everyone should just know telepathically what I needed, because I couldn't ask for help. This chronic imbalance would leave me feeling resentful and drained. I found this dimension incredibly painful. Sound familiar?

What I hadn't yet realized was that I was colluding with dysfunctional belief systems and inherited ancestral patterns, stuck in a victim mindset and co-creating my reality. How could I manifest love and support in my relationships if I didn't actually believe I deserved them?

Having ruminated on the idea of death for quite some time, one evening during a bout of suicidal ideation I began to write a bucket list. If I wasn't going to be here for very long anyway, I had nothing to lose, and I might as well do some of the things I really feared on the way out. Why not? I remember skydiving in the Arizona desert was one of them.

If you are feeling any of these feelings, please seek out the help of a trusted professional, friend or family member. Know that things can change and you are not alone.

As I continued to add adventures to my list, my mindset began to change. I asked God why we all had to suffer so much. In reply, to my surprise, I heard a string of answers that were spoken with total clarity: 'We are here to evolve. Make sure you cherish each new day, because we are here for the blink of an eye. And the soul is eternal.'

These are pretty simple concepts that you might be very familiar with, but we do forget them. And from that moment I have been grateful for the invisible riches that surround me every day.

Choosing to live was a massive turning point for me. I had been aware of angels as a child, and over the next year they reappeared in my life, and then the Divine Feminine showed up. I've never really spoken about this initiation, but she is at the very core of my work. The Divine Feminine is the Mother of all mothers. She lives in the land as Gaia, Pachamama and Mother Earth, but also exists as an inter-dimensional frequency of creation.

You're here to evolve.
Make sure you cherish each
new day because you're here
for the blink of an eye.
And the soul is eternal.

When we embody tenderness, gentleness, kindness, consistency, strength and compassion, we are diving into her slipstream of Love. She has many faces. In the early part of my life, she connected to me through Mother Mary and then Green Tara (the female bodhisattva), Mary Magdalene, Kwan Yin, Isis and Sophia (keeper of divine wisdom).

All of us, regardless of gender, have Divine Feminine and Divine Masculine aspects within us. It is part of our work here to activate and harmonize those energies. You don't need to believe in angels or even have heard of the Divine Feminine to do this work. I just invite you to stay curious and open. In my experience, when we connect with our own Divine Feminine aspect through our heart, our capacity to transform our blocks and heal our life is truly quantum.

•••

Alongside the spiritual experience, I was also having a human one. Growing up in my household was wild in all ways. As is so often the case with traumatized and emotionally immature parents who are traumatizing us, my mother could also embody the higher and more loving aspects of her soul energy. On the flipside of all the rage and drama was a courageous free-thinker with a razor-sharp psychic gift and a wicked sense of humour. By the age of 25, she had run a jazz club, lived on a houseboat in Paris, moved to London and was modelling to fund her backpacking adventures around the world!

She was a true child of the sixties, a daughter of the revolution, and like many of her generation, she had a deep desire to know God and make the world a better place. And so, together with a shedload of trauma to process, she also gifted me with a spiritual and esoteric education from a very early age.

I spent many hours during the first five years of my life at the Palace of Peace, an ashram in London. At that time, my mother had a guru called Maharaji, who hailed from Haridwar in northern India and had about a million followers worldwide. His devotees were called premies, taken from the Sanskrit word *prem*, which means 'love'.

We would all meet almost every evening for *satsang*, gathering to meditate and listen to Maharaji speak on different spiritual topics. I remember quite clearly that I wasn't convinced about his form of meditation, which involved putting pressure on the third eye with the middle finger. Or the request to kiss his feet. I'm not against kissing the feet of a holy person, but definitely not when the energy doesn't stack up. Those early years taught me about spiritual discernment and listening to your inner voice. You'll find some of the most self-involved egos in spiritual communities. Spiritual narcissism is very real!

It was at the Palace of Peace that my mum met Reg. They had a tumultuous and toxic relationship, but most weekends we would go on adventures, and our excursions were a deep education in themselves. Reg had a very powerful Druidic connection to the land. He could identify birdsong in the forest and we would visit sacred sites in wild places and walk along coastal paths and old Roman roads. Nature was always my refuge. She was a constant and kept me safe in the midst of it all.

At seven years old, I learned Transcendental Meditation, and would spend hours at the East London TM Centre, which was a rambling four-storey Victorian house a short walk from my home.

John Windsor ran the centre in a cosy way, surrounded by cats, big pots of tea and the antiques and collectables that he found rummaging through the local flea markets and charity shops. He was a kind man who had worked as a Fleet Street journalist before being invited to meet Maharishi Mahesh Yogi in the early 1970s. This was a few years after The Beatles had met Maharishi in Rishikesh, in northern India, catapulting TM onto the international stage.

This technique is based on ancient Vedic tradition and is non-religious, because it teaches that although 'Sages call it by various names... Truth is One' (Rig Veda). The Vedas – *veda* is Sanskrit for 'wisdom' – are sacred texts that form the foundation of Hindu philosophy, medicine and meditation. They were heard by sages after intense meditation and handed down as an oral tradition from 6000BCE before finally being written down between 1500 and 500BCE.

TM teaches the silent repetition of a mantra that induces relaxed brainwaves and moments of transcending. When we meditate, our brainwave frequency changes from beta to either alpha or theta, characterized by a relaxed inner wakefulness, stillness and feelings of creativity, bliss and peace.

The Vedas are based on the understanding that everything in existence is interconnected and beneath all thought is a unified field of consciousness where we are all One. The moments of transcending that are experienced when we practise meditation regularly are characterized by dropping into the quantum field, the field of pure consciousness.

What I have discovered through my healing work is that when we enter the chamber of the mystic heart, we are delivered to the same place.

Interestingly, practising this Vedic meditation technique led me into a close and deeply personal relationship with Christ. I met a girl called Tara at primary school and we would spend countless weekends together around the age of 10, slipping into many of the local Methodist and Baptist churches. The Caribbean ladies we met there disguised their bemusement with warm smiles and kind welcomes, cordially inviting us into their services. I recollect large, damp, echoey places with small but truly joyful congregations full of the spirit of God.

Then, in my late teens, I was introduced to a Sufi master and the time I spent in this community and tradition revealed how the journey to God, the Beloved, can only take place within the heart. This is where we share the ecstasy of union.

Whatever your understanding of God, if you like method, fact and proof, the universe, Divine Source or the Absolute can be a bit of a conundrum – an energetic body of light, Spirit, the 'something out there' that you may not wish to name but can feel from time to time. I have had the privilege of experiencing the beauty of many religions and shamanic traditions, and for me personally, there is only Source energy. Our holy books, rituals and practices simply offer us different ways to experience the Divine that is at the core of everything.

Let's take a moment now. Place both hands on your heart space, in the centre of your chest, close your eyes and take three deep breaths in through your nose, hold for a count of five and breathe out through your mouth.

Ask your heart what you believe in. It doesn't have to be 'spiritual' in any way. Perhaps you just believe in the power of Love, Light and good energy or people. Love is universal, after all.

'Everyone loves something, even if it's only tortillas.'
CHÖGYAM TRUNGPA

Write your heart findings in your journal.

Then close your eyes again, think of the words 'Source energy' and observe the images and words that arise for you. It's okay if you draw a blank or are unsure at this time. You're just beginning to take the first steps towards creating space for your heart to speak to you.

Dissolving the Defences

Aligning with heart energy, even for brief moments, has the power to dissolve the many ego-defences that we have used over time to shut down our heart and disconnect ourselves from our emotions.

There is a basic duality woven into the tapestry of existence. We embody two very distinct realities: a higher self and a lower self. The higher self is another way of describing our soul energy or True Essence. The lower self is often referred to as *the ego*. Many of us are completely unaware of the higher self, and in these cases the ego rules the roost!

The ego is transient. It is constructed in our formative years and belongs solely to this lifetime. If we were told we were clever, beautiful or worthy in childhood, our ego would have responded well. A nurturing childhood experience usually births a healthy ego that will support our deepest desires and dreams to a certain point. But all too often we use our ego like a shiny suit of armour to protect ourselves from criticism, shame and disappointment.

When we deepen our relationship with ourselves through our heart, however, we expand our capacity to manifest and experience functioning relationships with others. We no longer manifest emotional unavailability, because we learn to become more emotionally available to ourselves.

I have been called the heart whisperer, but I am here to teach you how to become your own whisperer. As you listen more to the murmurings of your heart and reclaim its immense power, your heart will teach you about true devotion. You will learn to cherish yourself with a new-found tenderness, and stand tall and know what authentic confidence and self-belief feel like.

> *'I listen with love to my inner voice.'*
> LOUISE HAY

For this, you have to be seen. I invite you to give permission for me to see you. We can start there. Just you and me. I am here to companion you back home and when you cross the line, you will learn how to companion yourself. Then you will become a companion to others. You will pay that love forward. It's just the way that Love operates. It's why we are here.

The Soul's Call

In the moments of our birth and death we are alone. Our time on the Earth plane is very short. The only real reason to be here is to love and be loved. It's that simple.

Perhaps pause here for a moment and reread those sentences. Breathe them in and breathe them out.

I have spoken those words many thousands of times in my sessions. I have repeated them like a mantra and they are yet to lose their relevance or potency for me. Often I find they bring a tear to my eye, as if I am speaking them for the very first time.

When I am sitting with a new client and these words shatter the glass walls of our shared expectant silence, I am actually throwing down the gauntlet. In medieval times, gauntlets were the heavy armoured gloves worn by the knights of the day, who would throw them to the ground when challenging someone to a duel. Today, the challenge is not an aggressive one, although there is most definitely a sense of urgency there.

At this specific time in humanity's history there is a very real need to hear and respond to that challenge. This is a time of great awakening, although a deep sense of confusion and forgetfulness also persists. As structures fall away, what is filling the void? We are at a crossroads, and each one of us has chosen this moment in our planet's evolution to be alive. We need to awaken together, 'one heart at a time'.

So now I am throwing down the gauntlet for you. Will you take up the challenge? Respond to the call? It is the call of your own soul, your True Essence, asking you to journey back to the divine vibration that you hold at the core of your being in your cosmic blueprint. That journey is woven into your destiny – and into our destiny and survival as a collective.

It calls for true intimacy.

In-to me-see.

If I let you see all of me, will you still love me?

Scary, isn't it?

Intimacy will feel like a radical concept if you've spent most of your life abandoning yourself and leaving yourself out in the cold. Many of us are doing this every day. If we've been emotionally or physically abandoned as children, we will automatically recreate that story in our adult life, because it's all we really know. The lie we tell ourselves is that it's not safe to be vulnerable and we subconsciously believe that 'in-to-me-see' will undoubtedly lead to deep hurt and painful rejection.

Growing up with a father who was emotionally absent, I learned to guard myself, to build walls around my vulnerability. This shield was both my armour and my prison, affecting everything from relationships to work, and laying a trail of destruction that spanned over three decades.

Jonathan

Expressing our genuine feelings, emotions, needs or boundaries is a real minefield when we live with a core, often subconscious belief that it's really not safe to communicate our truth. We will explore the impact of this later. For now, know that this belief really disrupts healthy communication in our relationships, because we haven't learned how to have robust intimate conversations and are terrified by the thought of being truly intimate with others for fear of what they could do to us.

We aren't even intimate with ourselves, because we haven't learned how to companion ourselves with compassion and love. We don't give ourselves a safe space to express all of our emotions and feelings. We are shut out of our emotional heart and whatever may reside in this chamber of our being.

When we are exiled from our heart, we can also feel at odds, or even at war with, our body. We are trapped in our mind, whirling away on a merry-go-round of incessant thoughts. It's like going through the motions of life but never truly touching down on Earth. Most people show up to my sessions this way, energetically 'out of body'. But when we connect with our True Essence, we embody it, and this is a game-changer. Being in our body means our deepest desires are supported by our *chi*, our life-force energy, which also turbo-charges our power to manifest the life of our dreams.

So, now I invite you to take both hands and place them in the middle of your chest, on your heart chakra, your heart energy centre, and repeat these words three times:

*'Today I give myself permission to be seen fully. I am
developing an intimate relationship with myself so
that I can become truly intimate with others. I am
choosing to companion myself. I am manifesting my
True Essence through my mystic heart. And so it is.'*

Write this affirmation down in your journal and begin your day with it. You don't need to be meditating to say these words to yourself. Repeat them when you're in the shower, brushing your teeth, making coffee, on the way back from the school run, sitting on the bus or going to work.

The Chambers of the Heart

It's by entering the chambers of the heart that we manifest our True Essence. Throughout history, prophets and sages have spoken about the energetic chambers of the heart that have been revealed to them spiritually. Esoteric traditions have passed the knowledge on. In the Sufi tradition there are five subtle bodies or chambers in the heart space. In Buddhism and Hinduism, the heart space is known as the Anahata chakra. It is the fourth chakra out of seven located in our energy body and it is the bridge between the upper and lower chakras, connecting the root, sacral and solar plexus with the throat, third eye and crown. It represents transformation, and the energy of love and compassion.

The heart, *hridayam*, is also known as the seat of the Self, *Atman* in Vedantic philosophy, and is the place of union with the Divine.

In the True Essence Process, as mentioned earlier, we imagine the heart as a series of three chambers: the physical chamber, the emotional chamber and the spiritual chamber.

Soul Wisdom and Cosmic Amnesia

When we tap into the power of our True Essence, we activate our soul wisdom. I believe that we arrive at the threshold of this life carrying our karma and an understanding of everything we have learned in our past lives. Our heart connects us with all of this hard-earned knowledge, which is stored in our cosmic DNA.

We are born into a family line, which creates a junction between an ancestral line and our own karmic line. We often choose a family lineage in order to engage with the specific lessons we require to clear our karma.

The minute we are birthed into this dimension, we experience what I call a type of 'cosmic amnesia'. But we all have unique coping mechanisms and gifts, although often it is our responsibility alone to excavate and claim those gifts.

When I am explaining this concept to my clients, I use the example of two brothers born to an alcoholic, physically abusive parent.

For one son, the experience impacts his ability to be in the world. He retreats from it and uses any form of addiction, from drugs and alcohol to food, gambling, porn and sex, to self-medicate. He seeks to avoid the immeasurable pain of his childhood trauma and subsequent chronic lack of self-esteem at all costs.

Meanwhile, back at the ranch of life, the other brother decides to kick against his childhood experience and use it to prove something to himself and the world. So, with the words 'I'll show you' metaphorically tattooed across his chest, he ends up as the CEO of a Fortune 100 company.

This doesn't make the CEO brother any better or worse than his sibling. It doesn't mean that he isn't suffering inside, although he may be unconscious of how much. And he certainly doesn't get to side-step the processing of that trauma at some point in his lifetime. No amount of money or status can ever buy a true sense of inner peace.

This story merely highlights how we come into the incarnation with different resources and sensitivities. Both brothers will eventually have to journey within if they wish to gain authentic mastery over their lives.

Escape into the Mind

Sadly, societal conditioning doesn't encourage us to go within. It has forced most of us out of our emotional heart, and the spiritual heart doesn't even make it into our collective awareness. We're taught from a very early age to escape into our mind and hunker down for the duration. We're like a ship that battens down the hatches when there's a storm on the horizon, except the storm becomes our whole life and we get stuck in a freeze, fight, flight or fawn state somewhere deep inside until we make a conscious choice to heal.

When you enter your emotional heart,

you can heal limiting beliefs and

clear the way for a direct connection

with your spiritual heart –

and your True Essence.

Expressing emotion is rarely modelled to us by our parents or caregivers in healthy, functional ways. There is a deep sense of shame and embarrassment associated with acknowledging or honouring any heartfelt experiences, and so we respond by shutting down our heart and end up feeling lost, empty or as if something is missing. Because it is.

If you can grieve for something you don't know you've lost, my whole being was grieving. My feelings of self-doubt, insecurity, anxiety, frustration and desperation hadn't come from my career, but from unconsciously never meeting myself. Bizarre, I know. How can you not know yourself in 31 years?

My desperate attempts to be accepted in every sense of the word had led me to morph into whoever I thought the world wanted me to be, so of course I had no idea what I wanted from life. I had never asked or allowed myself to answer the question before!

Elisha

Meanwhile, out there in the world, in our daily interactions, at work, on the street, in person, online, in the hustle and bustle of our routines and back-to back schedules, the energy of love gets a seriously bad rap. Our society's compulsive preoccupation with 'doing' rather than 'being' offers us the perfect opportunity to avoid the uncharted landscape of our inner world.

And so it really doesn't come as a great shock to find that we have disconnected from this fundamental lifeline gifted to us by the universe – our anchor and true north.

But you are being called back home in this moment. To a sense of embodied wholeness. To your original nature, your True Essence. So, allow your heart to soften and get ready to enter the first chamber. What will you discover?

Magic in Action

Heart energy is like the secret sauce. It's magic in action. When our heart softens and we access its energy, life is no longer just happening *to* us; instead we begin to *inhabit* each moment with a new sense of being.

And then, slowly but surely, a new voice emerges, saying – despite all of the old internal chatter – 'I deserve,' 'I belong,' 'I choose to receive.' More and more it will begin to say 'no' to the people, places and things that we don't like and 'yes' to the people, places and things that we do.

And as we grow more at ease with saying 'no', we create the mental space to really understand what our 'yes' is all about. What are the qualities we authentically desire and wish to manifest in our relationships, career or environment? What is our true passion? What is our purpose?

When we quit saying 'yes' to the wrong people for the wrong reasons, who are we becoming? We are becoming the architect of our own future. We are learning how to create magic in our own life.

The heart meditation is how we begin.

The Heart Meditation

Why meditation? There's a lot of hype around what it means to meditate and how to do it, but actually we can all meditate. It is embedded in our base-state programming. Our nine months in the womb are spent for the most part in a perfect meditative state. Just being... present... from one moment... to the next.

Meditation isn't complex. You can meditate with your eyes open, eyes closed, walking, sitting, lying, dangling upside down from the ceiling, in silence, dancing, chanting, guided, with music, inside, outside, whatever gets you there...

There are actually no rules, although daily practice is invaluable. It's like having a mobile phone charged to its full capacity. But it's not your best friend on the other side of town you're calling, it's your own heart, and beyond that the infinite field of consciousness.

So, just...

Begin by finding a quiet, comfortable place to sit or lie down.

Take both hands and place them in the middle of your chest, making sure your elbows and arms are completely relaxed.

Close your eyes, close your mouth, inhale through your nose and then open your mouth to exhale.

Keep breathing, really lengthening and deepening each inhalation into your solar plexus/stomach area and opening your mouth wide and sinking each exhalation into your solar plexus.

Lengthening your breath engages your parasympathetic nervous system, which slows down your heart rate and supports a feeling of safety in your body.

Notice if you are holding your breath in your upper body, and if so, allow it to soften into your body.

With each breath, give yourself permission to arrive in the space more.

Allow yourself to arrive fully.

Take your time.

Breath by breath, every part of you arrives.

You are working with breath, a very powerful energy, the invisible thread of life that *separates you from death in this moment*, and in this moment, set the intention to rest your physical body... the bones of this incarnation...

We will use visualization during this meditation. Don't overthink it. Allow the images to form effortlessly.

Give permission for your physical body to completely relax as you work with your spiritual and emotional bodies in this session.

On your next breath, bring your awareness to your facial muscles and imagine them softening as you untie your mask, the mask that you present to the world.

Remove it completely, so that your face can truly relax.

Notice the sounds in the room and outside the room – cars, people, lives... the many hundreds, thousands and millions of lives on the outside...

And then bring yourself back to the breath inside you.

Bring yourself back to the constant rise and fall of life-force energy in the midst of it all... in the midst of the to-ing and fro-ing of life...

On the next breath, bring your attention to your heart, bringing your breath to your heart as a gift... a gift of love.

And in this moment, give permission for your heart to exhale whatever it chooses to exhale... You don't even need to know what it is.

You are spending a few moments with your heart... honouring all that you *have* loved, all that you *do* love and all that you *will* love.

You are honouring your heart's profound capacity to love, right at the centre of this incarnation, pushing love around the incarnation, and right at the centre of this body, pushing life around the body.

Use the next exhalation to drop down into your heart a little bit more. Trust the exhalation. The exhalation will get you there.

You can imagine that you're climbing down into a cave... the cave of self. With each exhalation, you're climbing down a little bit more... really noticing where you are and how deep this place is within you.

In the darkness, find the handle to a door. Turn the handle and open the door to reveal a room of light – bright white light. It's enough to just imagine it...

Step over the threshold, from the darkness into the light. Notice the shift in energy as the light washes through you like a wave, a tsunami of light... and feel yourself absorbing that light into every cell of your body... into your eyes, nose, hair and thousands of skin cells... absorbing the light more deeply... into your capillaries and arteries... into your blood... into every organ in your body... your brain, your larynx, your heart, your lungs, your upper and lower intestines, your liver, kidneys, gall bladder, bladder, spleen, pancreas, sexual organs... and more deeply... into your bones, your bone marrow.

In the centre of this room, know that you are in a room of infinite rooms of infinite light that exist *right here, right now* in the universe... oceans and oceans and *oceans* of infinite light... right at the centre of your *being*...

Take some time to reflect on what emerged during this meditation.

Journal Prompts

* Describe how it felt when you first encountered your heart space. Was there any resistance? Write down any thoughts or sensations that you experienced.

* As you were visualizing climbing down on each exhalation, you were accessing the chamber of your emotional heart. What did you feel there? Was there a sense of grief, relief, overwhelm, joy – all or none of the above?

* The room of light is your spiritual/mystic heart. Did you make it over the threshold of this room? What images, feelings or bodily sensations did you experience in this chamber?

I am sitting in session with a new client. We have just completed the opening meditation and dropped into heart space together.

This is a truly liminal place, between dimensions. In it, I download a series of images, names or words that build a picture of the specific chapter in the client's history that their 'family in the light' have decided needs to be attended to first. In this initial session, they give me very clear ages when there have been psychological 'breaks' or ruptures in the client's childhood. These breaks are moments of defining trauma and are generally at the root of the blocks that are experienced in adulthood.

We all have a family in the light, which I have found includes a guardian angel, deceased family members, ancestors, guides and animals, either spirit ones or pets that we have known and loved over the course of our lifetime. You will meet some members of your own family in the light on your journey to manifesting your True Essence. They will be your allies along the way, a support group when you need one, friends and fellow travellers.

When I am with a client, I also receive information from my personal guides, and we all come together to co-create a safe alchemical container for the work. This is a portal of sorts, where it is possible for my client to really feel the power of their emotional heart and glimpse something of their True Essence.

There is often a cheer or a 'Hallelujah!' in the spirit world in these initial sessions when a client connects with the truth of who they are beneath their pain and suffering. It is a reminder of where we're going, of the alchemical gold at the end of this rainbow, of the return to wholeness, the return to Love.

For all of us, when we pray, chant, meditate, repeat affirmations or allow the feeling of love to flood our systems through our heart, even for brief moments, the energy of each cell changes its vibration accordingly. We become more grounded. We feel protected and safe. And when we feel safe, a deeper sense of calm gently begins to permeate our daily activities.

By creating these pockets of sacred space within the maelstrom of our busy lives, we're plugging ourselves *into the most powerful energy supply imaginable*. We are aligning ourselves to the infinite oceans of light energy that exist in the unseen world. *Right here. Right now.*

So, make time to plug into that heart energy daily.

Why a Daily Practice?

'Be courageous and discipline yourself.
Work. Keep digging your well.
Don't think about getting off from work.
Submit to a daily practice.
Your loyalty to that is a ring on the door.
Keep knocking, and the joy inside
will eventually open a window
and look out to see who's there.'

RUMI

Our ego tells us that we're broken if we are unable to make grand gestures of love in this life, the gestures that society recognizes as marriage or having children. But whilst these form powerful bedrocks for understanding the many faces of love, some of the most seemingly mundane day-to-day events can suffuse our being with love. And it is that energy alone that has the power to radically transform and heal.

So, can you stop along the way to see heaven in a wildflower, or look up and take a few moments to appreciate the splendid hues of a setting sun above an urban landscape? How about caring for your pet? Sitting with a purring cat or walking a dog? Or greeting an older person who lives on your street? Saving hedgehogs might be your thing, or gardening. These are glimmers, or moments of gratefulness, which we will be exploring in more detail later in the journey.

Whatever it is, do it daily to support the rewiring of new neural pathways. Yes, the human brain has the power to change itself.

*'Neural plasticity exists from the cradle to the grave, and
practicing a new skill, under the right conditions, can
change hundreds of millions and possibly billions of the
connections between the nerve cells in our brain maps.'*
NORMAN DOIDGE

Daily practice is an important way of embodying your new understandings of the heart, of shifting them from the realm of thought and concept into the real world – from the head into the body.

As you awaken more, there will come a time when many of these heart tools will be fully integrated into everything that you do.

For now, here are some practices to incorporate into your day.

Thank Your Physical Heart

Begin by taking your awareness into the lower region of your stomach. Breathe deeply into the area below your belly button three times. As you inhale, feel your whole upper body expanding.

In your mind's eye, see your chest area opening.

As you exhale, imagine you are slowly pushing your breath to the opposite wall. If you are lying down, imagine it is touching the ceiling.

Close your eyes and breathe into your physical heart. There is no right or wrong way to do this. This is your breath. Your heart. Your moment.

Use your imagination to take yourself into the organ itself. The lifeline. *Your* lifeline. Be conscious of the energy of gratefulness. Breathe gratefulness into your physical heart.

Breathe the words, 'Heart, I am truly grateful for all the work you do. Your constancy. Your power.'

Open a Dialogue
with Your Emotional Heart

Every day, give your emotional heart the opportunity to speak through the practices below. At first there may only be a word or two, but soon there will be more, many more.

Some of you may already have a morning ritual; add this heart diary work to that time. If you don't have one, wake up 10 minutes earlier or find some time in the evening to create sacred space for yourself. How?

~ Light a candle, burn some incense, sage or resin and affirm that you are opening sacred space in order to meet your True Essence.

~ Place both hands in the middle of your chest, on your heart chakra, and take three long deep breaths into that space. You can repeat the heart meditation from this chapter if you have time, or just work with your breath for a few moments, focusing on feeling your heart expanding with each breath.

~ Ask your heart what it is feeling or holding.

~ Listen and your heart will speak to you. Write down the reply as a stream of consciousness in your journal.

_____

'Be soft in your practice. Think of the method as a
fine silvery stream, not a raging waterfall.'
SHENG YEN

'Connected, grounded, aligned, at peace with my soul – all of this and
more is what I gained over the following weeks of listening to my heart.'
ELISHA

CHAPTER 3

Alchemy of the Heart

*'You are beauty incarnate.
There is gold buried within you.'*

You might be asking the questions: 'Why the heart?' and 'What is alchemy?' It's not common knowledge that the heart is a treasure trove of wonder. Most people believe it is a physical organ whose sole purpose is to pump blood around the body as instructed by the brain. It *is* a physical organ, of course, and we can so easily forget the beauty of the physical heart and how it serves us so profoundly for our entire time here on the Earth plane, so let's start with a reminder.

The Physical Heart

Just to get a little bit of perspective on the 'wow' factor of the physical heart, it is the first organ to form in the embryo, generating electricity and power and sustaining life. It consists of four chambers: an atrium and ventricle on both its right and left sides. In very simple terms, the right side of the heart receives blood that is low in oxygen, which is then pumped into the lungs, where it is fully oxygenated again. This blood is then pumped through the left-hand side of the heart to nourish the rest of the body.

The physical heart beats between 70 to 80 times per minute, circulating a gallon and a half of blood around the body, which is approximately 2,000 gallons a day. This works out at a staggering 58 million gallons over a lifetime. Our entire cardiovascular system, which is made up of the heart, blood vessels, arteries, veins and capillaries, is 60,000 miles long and could wrap itself around the planet 2.5 times. On a purely physical level alone, the heart is truly mind-blowing!

Maybe take a moment to touch your heart gently with your fingertips, appreciate the wonder of it, and take a deep breath and say, 'Thank you.'

In the 1960s and 70s husband-and-wife team John and Beatrice Lacey were at the cutting edge of physiology, psychology and heart research. They were the first to discover that the heart was in a continual dialogue with the brain.

> *'It was found that the heart seemed to have its own*
> *peculiar logic that frequently diverged from the*
> *direction of the autonomic nervous system. The heart*
> *appeared to be sending meaningful messages to the*
> *brain that it not only understood, but also obeyed.'*
> LACEY AND LACEY

By the early 1990s, Canadian neurologist Dr Andrew Armour had found that the heart contained a sophisticated collection of 40,000 neurons that organized themselves into a small but complex nervous system. In 1991, he coined the term 'heart brain':

*'The heart's brain is an intricate network of several types
of neurons, neurotransmitters, proteins and support cells
similar to those found in the brain proper. Its elaborate
circuitry enables it to act independently of the cranial
brain – to learn, remember, and even feel and sense.'*

Traditional neuroscience regards memory as a function of the brain, not the heart, but neurocardiology has now discovered that the heart also has a memory. Maybe pause to really allow that news to land: the heart has a memory, so among other things it can actually remember events in your life. This explains why some of the recipients of heart transplants have experienced changes in their tastes, preferences and lifestyle related to their donors.

In her book *A Change of Heart*, Claire Sylvia wrote about her experience after a heart and lung transplant. Claire was a 47-year-old dancer and choreographer who, after surgery, noticed changes in her cravings and personality traits. Suddenly she had hankerings for chicken nuggets and beer. She became impetuous, started to walk like a man and was attracted to curvaceous blonde women.

Five months later, she had an extraordinary dream about a thin young man called Tim L., who had died in a motorcycle accident at the age of 18. She woke up with no doubt that this was her donor: 'Some parts of his spirit and personality were now in me.'

Some years later, she discovered Tim's obituary in a newspaper and found his family. Everything she had felt about him was true.

Heart Coherence

Not only does the heart have a cellular memory, but science has also discovered that when it is in a coherent state, i.e. calm and balanced, its frequency is 0.1Hz, which is the same as one of the Earth's primary resonant frequencies.

Neurocardiology research has revealed more about the heart's electro-magnetic energy too. In the 1960s, scientists pioneered a technique to measure the magnetic fields produced by the heart's electrical currents and found that the heart generated an electromagnetic field that extended three feet around the body in all directions and was a staggering 100 times more powerful than that of the brain. Wherever you are, whatever you are doing, the invisible force of energy that is created by your heart can be felt by others.

Science has also found that prayer engages the heart centre and its power is real. When groups of people come together in prayer, meditation or other spiritual practices, the electromagnetic vibrations generated circulate into the collective consciousness, co-creating renewal and recovery.

How does this work? A photon is a tiny light particle made up of electro-magnetic waves. It is believed that the average person emits 20 photons of light per second. Research has shown that when we meditate on our heart centre whilst directing love and light to others, we emit 100,000 photons of light per second.

The Heart-Mind

The heart communicates with the brain not only electromagnetically, but also through nerve impulses, hormones, neurotransmitters and pressure waves. Recent research by the HeartMath Institute in California has confirmed that the heart sends more signals to the brain than the other way around.

The heart generates a magnetic field 100 times more powerful than the field produced by the brain. Wherever you are, whatever you're doing, the invisible force of energy that's created by your heart can be felt by others.

These heart signals have a significant effect on brain function, influencing creativity and emotional processing as well as cognitive faculties such as attention, perception, memory and problem-solving.

What this means in simple terms is that the heart is actually an information-processing centre with a very powerful mind of its own. This is called the heart-mind, and you have already begun the practice of checking in with it every day. Now, choose to activate and engage with it more. On the way to work or in your lunch break could be a good time.

If you can't place your hands on your heart, it also works to bring your focus to the centre of your chest. Take three deep breaths into that space and tell your heart you're giving permission for it to express its full truth.

Listen and your heart-mind will speak to you more and more. Write the communication down in your journal.

You are developing a new skill here by learning to hold space for your heart whilst not being overtaken by the feelings it's holding.

A Universal Touchstone

Although in the modern world we have almost completely lost sight of the true power of the heart, from the dawn of human civilization through millennia and across cultures and religions, the heart was our touchstone. The first *Homo sapiens* to settle in Europe before the last Ice Age, 48,000 years ago, were featuring the symbol of the heart in the pictograms they were painting onto cave walls. In a very primal and instinctive way, our ancient ancestors really understood that the beating heart signified life itself. They observed how our heartbeat would begin to race if we were experiencing either fear or excitement and cease forever when our time in this dimension was done.

The ancient Egyptians believed that all things emanated from the heart, not the brain. It was central to emotion, intellect, memory and personality. But perhaps most importantly for the early Egyptians, it was the seat of the soul. This is why during the mummification process, all the other organs were removed and the heart was left intact – to take into the afterlife.

According to Egyptian mythology, at the moment of death the god Anubis would lead the soul to the Hall of Two Truths. Here, Osiris, lord of the underworld, would place the heart on one side of a set of golden scales, with the white feather of the goddess Ma'at, symbolizing cosmic justice, balance and truth, on the other. If your heart balanced the feather, you were granted access to the paradisical Field of Reeds. However, if your heart was burdened with the weight of sin and corruption, it was thrown to the ground and devoured by Amenti, a god with the face of a crocodile, the front of a leopard and the back of a rhinoceros. This would eradicate your soul from existence, which was the most unthinkable of punishments for the ancient Egyptians, a fate far worse than death.

In Buddhism, ultimate enlightenment is reached through the integration of one of the most famous Buddhist scriptures, the Heart Sutra, whilst in ancient India the heart was the cradle of the soul and our intelligence – it was recognized as the home of the 'self'. The ancient Hindu text Atharva Veda (1100BCE) describes the heart as a lotus with nine gates or openings. It was the link between heaven and Earth, the place where the love of Brahman was experienced. The Chandogya Upanishad in the Sama Veda (800BCE) speaks of 'The innermost heart', being 'greater than the earth, greater than the mid-region, greater than heaven. This Soul, this self of mine, is that of Brahman.'

In ancient Greece, the philosopher Aristotle would later declare that the heart was the seat of the soul and observed how it was the first organ to form in the body, whilst Traditional Chinese medicine has always heralded it as the Emperor organ, and home to our *shen* or spirit.

So, over the years, the power of the heart has been recognized many times. Not only has the heart been the focal point for our most elevated emotions and spiritual aspirations, but it has also captured our imagination in a truly profound way, inspiring the world's greatest music, poetry, art and literature.

The heart speaks the universal language of love, compassion, moral courage and truth.

It is at the core of our humanity.

It is the space where alchemy happens.

• • •

That's something I know well today, but back in my twenties, the last thing I wanted to do was to become a professional healer or psychic. At that time, if you meditated on a regular basis, ate brown rice or enjoyed the odd tree hug, let alone if you also felt 'energy' and happened to speak to dead people, society had a lot to say about you, and none of it was particularly polite! Whilst each and every one of us is a light being, and remembering our True Essence is what this lifetime is all about, it hasn't been encouraged by society.

Also, it's quite common to carry an unconscious wound related to our past lives. Think for a moment about how we've brutalized and judged one another in the name of religion and tradition for millennia. At any one time, depending on the year or the century, we have demonized and utterly terrorized one another for the different ways we have chosen to meet the Divine. Even when we've been members of the same religion!

Perhaps you were once a hermit in the caves of India or Asia. Or maybe a nun or a monk following any one of the monastic traditions, from Buddhism to Christianity. Or a herbalist living on the edge of a village, or a wise woman or man. The healer/medicine/shaman/witch wound is very real. And it absolutely resonates with me. I can almost taste the lives when I've been punished for not conforming to society's rules and regulations. So much so that even when I stepped over the line and dedicated my life to this work, I still didn't have a website for years.

So, rewind to the 20-something me. She wasn't remotely interested in explaining or defending herself, or taking on the responsibility of healing. There was something about the blend of my astrological chart – Aries Sun, Sagittarius Moon, Virgo rising – coupled with my own childhood story and personality that gave me the feeling that it would be hardcore, and I just wasn't up for it.

I just wanted to be 'normal' and have an adventure totally unrelated to how I'd grown up. My dream job at that time was to become a television and radio host, so, using what I innately understood about manifestation, which I will share with you through this process, I focused all my energy on that goal and turned my dream into reality.

Those years were a very blessed time in my life. At one point I was working on three travel shows at once, which was my idea of heaven. I travelled to the most beautiful cities and most remote corners of the planet. I journeyed to deserts, oceans, jungles and snow-capped mountain ranges – everywhere from Rome and Istanbul to Iceland, Australia, Africa and Pakistan. It was such a privilege to explore and experience so much of the world, its history, cultures and spiritual traditions. And a truly precious gift to spend time with so many wonderful people.

One day, in the midst of jetting around the globe, I got a very strong message from Spirit that the father of my child was not in England. I was guided to pack my bags and move to America. And I listened. I have always trusted the wisdom of my inner voice. Being able to distinguish between the voice of your higher self and your ego really helps you make some of the decisions in life that will help manifest the change that you are dreaming about. By the time you've finished reading this book, my hope is that you will have connected to your higher self and feel fully confident to follow your heart.

I followed mine, and just a few years later I was heavily pregnant and living with my son's father under the Hollywood sign in Los Angeles. And then God said, 'Okay, Estelle, it's time for you to step up.'

I do believe you can run but you can't hide. We often try to do that with our healing. We think that if we look in the other direction and walk away from it, we'll manage to side-step the work. The same can be said for elements of our destiny. We may fancy a bit of a rest, but there will be a handful of 'purpose projects' that we need to action in this incarnation and our soul will be looking to tick these experiences off the karma list.

So, I gave my ego a good talking-to, got out of the way of myself and surrendered to my purpose. Los Angeles is super-haunted and our apartment building was full of spooks, so I cleared it. Then people started arriving by word of mouth on my doorstep for readings and healing. When my son was a toddler, I found that I could work around his childcare. Having a healing practice worked really well with being a new mum. I trusted the guidance and surrendered to what was being presented to me.

'You are encircled by the arms of the Mystery of God.'
HILDEGARD OF BINGEN

As I began working more regularly and consciously chose to be of service, the Divine Feminine guided me more deeply. I've already mentioned this energy and the fact that we all have Divine Feminine and Divine Masculine aspects within us. We express the Divine Feminine through intuition, flow, surrender, nurture, reflection, communication, creativity and empathy.

In my one-to-one healing sessions and then later at my retreats, I was guided by the Divine Feminine to the three chambers of the heart. Everything begins and ends there for me, and I have now dedicated my life to the alchemical power of the heart.

The Great Work

Our soul is a nugget of the most beautiful gold. And our life is spent panning for that nugget. Sifting the debris from the precious metal. The wheat from the chaff. Allowing the gold to shine. This is the alchemy of the heart.

The ability to 'sift' is essential. We so easily forget that being perfect was never part of the agreement that we made before we decided to come back to Earth. If we were perfect, we just wouldn't be here! We'd be wafting about in a light dimension. So, we all have our own debris to clear – mountains of the stuff! The debris is a manifestation of our own personal karma. But beneath it is the gold of who we really are. Medieval alchemists called the process of unearthing that gold 'the Great Work'. They were searching for the Philosopher's Stone, the elixir of life, which contained the secret of immortality.

Imagine a 15th-century alchemist's workshop, with piles of leather-bound books, shelves of potions and a big bubbling experiment on an old oak table in the centre of the room. The purpose of the experiment is to turn one metal into another metal. To turn lead into gold.

Alchemists spent many a long night looking for the secret that would bring about this transformation on a physical level. But they also used the process as an analogy for soul development: transforming a heavy base metal into the purest, brightest and most valued of all metals.

Base Metal

Before we begin the process of becoming more self-aware, our energy is dense and heavy like the base metal lead.

People who come to see me are often deeply perplexed as to why they are unable to manifest abundance in either their relationships, their career or their creativity. Sometimes all areas are blocked. Other times success may be evident on the surface, but there's pain on the inside.

'I'm stuck' is something I hear a lot. 'It feels like I'm trying to push water uphill.' 'I never meet the right partner.' 'It feels as though I'm walking through treacle.' 'Nothing ever falls into place for me.' And so on and so forth!

'If you could just take a look at those hugely unattractive lead boots that you're wearing,' I say, 'you'd see why. What would you expect from the energy of abundance when you're sporting footwear like that?'

I explain that like is attracted to like. So the energy of abundance is attracted to like energy. Or at least energy on the move. How can you move in lead boots?

The boots are a metaphor for the unprocessed thoughts and emotions that hold us back from success, peace, joy... and of course *love*. To live in *love* means to live without fear. To *trust*. And, like the perfect chrysalis unfolding, in that state all timing is perfect. Where before there were obstacles and confusion, now there is newfound clarity, along with unbending support for all that we do.

The time has come for you to trip
the light fantastic in the most perfect
pair of specially designed golden
slippers. Or perhaps to lose the
footwear altogether – to go barefoot,
grow some wings and take off.

Thankfully, as you're reading this book, the time has come for you to take the boots off.

'This is Love: to fly toward a secret sky,
to cause a hundred veils to fall each moment.
First, to let go of life. Finally, to take a step without feet.'
RUMI

Actually you can wear whatever you like – gold-encrusted platforms, thigh-high boots, flip-flops. Just make sure you ditch the lead and join me on this alchemical adventure.

I am sitting with Pete for the first time. His wife has sent him to me and insisted that I see him sooner rather than later, as he hasn't been doing very well. Pete is a 41-year-old father of two. He works in sales and also runs a small bed and breakfast from his house on the outskirts of London.

As I explained earlier, when I am working with a new client I receive a specific set of 'notes' for them. This information drops into my consciousness and I read it just as a doctor might read a patient's notes at the end of a hospital bed. I get the key ages when trauma has impacted the lifetime and also the relationships that have shaped the person's ability to successfully manifest intimacy, joy and abundance.

Pete is no exception, and I read that his relationship with his mother has defined the shape and texture of his block and we need to focus on his 12-year-old self.

At 12, Pete found out that his mother had cancer, and from that moment onwards he took it upon himself to protect his sisters and hold the family together. When his mother passed away when he was 16, he was never given the space or time to grieve. And that pattern is now impacting everything. Not only is he suffering from physical pain, but he is also the prisoner of a self-perpetuating cycle of co-dependency, disassociation, anger and resentment with his partner and children. Zero joy.

No one asked Pete how he was feeling at any moment during the years of his mother's illness or after her death, and he responded by completely shutting down his heart energy and constructing an internal 'panic room' to navigate his terror and anguish. No one has ever been permitted to enter that panic room, and Pete's highly effective masking techniques have been so masterful that he believes that no one even knows he has one.

But I do. Spirit has shown me a padded room. A cell. A toxic control-room. And when I ask Pete what he is feeling in there, tears begin to slowly emerge, but he has no language for his emotion.

'I don't know,' he keeps repeating. 'I'm not sure why I'm crying. I just don't know.'

'Your heart will tell you, Pete,' I say gently. 'Ask your heart.'

And so he does. He places both his hands on his heart chakra, closes his eyes and deepens his breath.

'Fear,' he replies after a few moments, with a certainty that only the emotional heart will provide. 'Sadness and helplessness.'

'What Happened to You?'

We very rarely ask each other the very basic question: 'What happened to you?' No one had asked Pete this question.

I have found in my work that tuning in to what has happened to us and communicating with our emotional heart has the power to dynamically access our historical trauma and rapidly alchemize it.

There are many definitions of trauma in psychotherapy, psychiatry and neuroscience, but Dr Peter Levine's explanation really resonates with me: 'Trauma is experiencing fear in the face of helplessness.' Physiologically, the body goes into a fight, flight, freeze or fawn response, and if we aren't able to process our feelings at the time, the energy of that traumatic event is stored in our body.

As Levine explains:

> *'Studies show that naming your emotions immediately*
> *releases their grip over you and reduces physiological distress.*
> *Emotional labeling provides emotional clarity, giving you a*
> *deeper understanding of what happened and how it affects*
> *you and helps you see the possibilities of what to do next.'*

Understanding what has happened to us and how it affects us leads to a greater level of self-acceptance and creates the space for powerful healing to happen.

I recently facilitated a two-week workshop for a group of young people who had attempted suicide at least once and had a history of chronic self-harm. They had all experienced some form of childhood trauma and had difficulty managing their distress, understanding their emotions and building relationships.

In the first session, breathing mindfully into the heart proved to be incredibly challenging, confronting and uncomfortable for them.

They came back the following week and we created an artwork depicting how their hearts had begun a very new dialogue with them. There was a humbling resilience in the room.

One of the girls had suffered from a heart condition that meant that not only had she shut down her emotional heart, but she was completely disconnected from her physical heart too. At the end of the final day, she wrote:

> 'With the trauma from my physical heart, I lost sight of my emotional heart. The passion and longing from my inner child and "putting heart into what I do" became lost and shadowed by the grief of my illness. However, during the session, I experienced a catharsis and realized that the heart with which I love is still there. I let go of the weight of the world and opened my emotional heart again.'

Great Work Amnesia

One thing is for sure: most of us are suffering from a very bad case of Great Work amnesia. We just seem to forget that this life is an exceptional gift. It's a chance for *us* to be exceptional. But we forget or don't believe that it's our 'lot' to be or do anything that could ever be described that way.

I just want to get one thing straight: each and *every* one of us – bar *none* – has the opportunity to be *great*. To be *gold*. In our own unique way.

So, why not give yourself permission to do just that? Right here, right now. It needn't be too radical. Just give yourself permission to press the 'mute' button inside your head and quieten that critical voice for the time it takes you to get to the end of this chapter. For a moment in time, just suspend the chatter that rattles on incessantly about you not being good enough, not being clever, pretty, fit or wealthy enough – low-level, often inaudible chatter, but chatter all the same. Mute it now! And read on...

Yes, it's true that we're not all cut out to lead nations or head up huge corporations. You may not have the slightest inclination to find the cure for society's greatest woes or to be the next Nobel Prize winner, but don't think that lets you off the cosmic hook. There will still be a unique 'something' that only you can do. And it's enough. It's more than enough.

If you don't know what that your 'thing' is yet, give yourself permission to remember. If you do know, honour that gift. Honour it by choosing to express it.

The practice of tuning in to a particular quality, skill or talent will remind you of your uniqueness and get the cogs of your heart moving. It will create space for the alchemy to happen.

Pearls

Consider this: how does a pearl become a pearl?

It doesn't necessarily follow that at the bottom of the ocean inside a fairly unremarkable-looking seashell something extraordinary is happening. But sometimes it is. A piece of grit is being transformed into a pearl.

This is another way of looking at the alchemical process. In life, the good and bad medicine administered by the people we meet along the way provides us with the much-needed 'grit' that will rub the pearl of our soul back into being. This invaluable process is a journey that returns us to our original nature – to our mystical heart, our True Essence. We just need to be open to it.

I attended Estelle's Love Retreat at the end of my tether, fraught with depression and anxiety. Every day I felt very low, and it had been with me for some months. I was already on antidepressants, yet still so depressed. The holistic good stuff – diet, counselling, yoga, meditation and exercise – they just weren't helping. I had suicidal thoughts, an extreme manifestation of the pain I was in. I felt ready to do anything to relieve myself of it.

I arrived at the venue flustered, rushed, irritable. My driven, organized and impatient mind began the weekend ready for the end. Already angry for no reason. 'Okay, let's go. What's happening now? When does the healing begin? When will this pain stop?' Anger and impatience were my self-protection shields, because deep down I was frightened and desperate.

Estelle builds the stages of the retreat slowly, but with high expectations of everyone from the outset. You commit unquestionably to the trust work. It makes you feel so vulnerable to open up your heart to strangers, to embrace the immediate readiness required of you and others to share and witness your truth. We learned about one another's deepest pain. But in that intimate space, surrounded by women doing the same, you realize you're so very far from alone. In fact, your story is familiar, universal. We are all the same. We all deserve love, and we all need to love ourselves more.

The day before the healing day, still in my impatient, expectant, demanding mode, I asked Estelle if she knew of any energy healers in the local area I could book a session with before heading home.

She looked at me, very surprised. Then, with a wry smile, she said, 'Wait until tomorrow, then ask me.'

I had no idea what was coming.

It's hard to explain what unfolded on the healing day. As a group, we later agreed it would be almost impossible to fully describe it to others. You had to live it to believe it. Every individual's session was unique. Our order was random (or was it?) and the approach, the layout, the formation, the music, the connection, the process, the response... were all different.

I panicked and ran before mine.

Estelle gently challenged me: 'You're free to go home. Or choose to be rid of this.'

I chose to live. That meant staying and facing it head on.

For months it had felt as if a large rock, or small bowling ball, was sitting on my throat, crushing my lower windpipe. It was a constant and unrelenting fixture of physical discomfort. I felt as if I couldn't breathe. It was at its worst as I entered the healing space.

The experience was almost too much to share, let alone be believed. But I know in that healing session Estelle physically managed to move 'something' from my stomach, through my chest, up my windpipe and out of my mouth – a cloud, a fog, a darkness. It felt physical, visceral, and immediately the weight on my throat was gone. My chest felt lighter. My breathing was deeper.

The experience brought profound realizations. One of the key discoveries: I was brought up in London in a proud Scottish household. From a young age

I figured out I could switch my accent and was compelled to do so, to fit in and feel the same as those around me.

The routine stuck; it became part of me into adulthood. Always adapting, complying and masking, in an effort to be accepted. At times it felt performative and inauthentic. I didn't know who I was, or wanted to be, or what was real and true for me.

The Love Retreat lifted the weight of caring about others' opinions of me, especially in regard to my own voice, my foundation of self-expression.

Having arrived at the retreat a 'Londoner', I joined the group after breakfast the morning after my healing and decided I'd speak to them in the accent I felt most comfortable in: my Scottish accent.

Needless to say, it caused a riot of love, laughter, support and celebration. The 'real me' was awakened. I re-introduced myself and felt proud – proud of who I was at my most comfortable and authentic.

The 'bowling ball' weight on my throat has never returned.

Liz

> *'Your task is not to seek for love, but merely to seek and find all the barriers within yourself that you have built against it.'*
> RUMI

Rumi didn't become the greatest mystic poet in history overnight. It was his life's purpose, but it wasn't until his late thirties, when he met the Sufi philosopher and mystic Shams Tabrizi, aka 'the bird', that he stepped fully into his power and became all that he had originally signed up to become.

Shams reminded him about love. The two years that they spent together were about exploring separation, union and the ecstasy of love. In Sufism, the mystical seeker is the lover and God is the Beloved.

Creating Space for Love

*'The minute I heard my first love story I started looking
for you, not knowing how blind that was.
Lovers don't finally meet somewhere.
They're in each other all along.'*

RUMI

Ultimately, it will be your very own ability to *love*, and love again and again, that will render you utterly speechless and truly humbled. To *love oceans of infinite love* is the great lightbulb moment.

But first...

Take a few moments now to imagine yourself at the wheel of a fabulous sailing ship.

This ship looks like something out of *Pirates of the Caribbean*. It has huge white linen sails billowing in the wind and polished mahogany decking underfoot.

The ship is in the middle of the ocean and you've just spotted the most beautiful bay on the horizon. Land ahoy! White sands, palm trees and the promise of some really good times are staring you in the face.

Things are looking up for once, so you head for the shore... Bring it on!

But then you look up and suddenly you're back out at sea again.

How did that happen? Well, your lower decks are so full that you can never really make any headway. Real progress is elusive, and you'll often find you end up with similar outcomes or back at square one.

At some point your ship will start sinking too if you don't begin the process of clearing your lower decks. The time has come to cut loose and finally release some of the 'unprocessed baggage' down there.

What might be in that unprocessed baggage? Layers of old emotions will be there, for sure. Our emotions colour the way we think about absolutely everything in our lives, and our thoughts have the power to shape reality. When our emotions are frayed, damaged or disturbed, the path to manifesting authentic joy will be compromised.

So, to complete the Great Work, we must first transform our emotions. Then, when we have alchemized all that is held in our emotional heart, we can enter our mystic heart and discover the wisdom of our True Essence.

To alchemize our emotions, we first have to know what they are. We have to seek them out. We have to enter the Shadowlands...

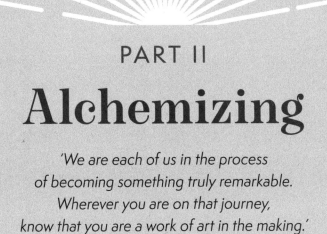

PART II

Alchemizing

'We are each of us in the process
of becoming something truly remarkable.
Wherever you are on that journey,
know that you are a work of art in the making.'

CHAPTER 4

The Shadowlands

'To light a candle is to cast a shadow.'
Ursula K. Le Guin

By softening and opening your heart, you've already opened a portal of possibility. Softening our heart expands our consciousness. It helps us stay open to how life could change and how *we* have the power to change it.

Know that your emotional heart is *so* relieved that you've chosen to heal. I can't emphasize that fact enough at this stage, because you won't quite be reaping the benefits yet, but trust that they're coming. In the meantime, stay curious to the rich textures and gifts of your emotional heart and the Shadowlands that we're about to visit together.

This might be your first introduction to the idea of having a Shadow side, or you may have worked with your Shadow in some capacity before. Wherever you find yourself on that journey, we're all starting anew here, because we're meeting the Shadow through the power of the heart and not through logic or the mind.

Remember that you're going home. You're returning to your authentic nature, a sense of embodied wholeness, a cradle of love, your True Essence, and to get there you need to alchemize some of what your emotional heart is holding for you.

Wherever you are right now, reading or listening to these words, know that you have everything you need to do this and... you're doing great!

Dismantling the Fortress

As children, we build a wall around our emotional heart when we feel unseen or unheard in our family or childhood environments. Every time we suffer rejection, abandonment, hurt or physical, psychological, emotional or sexual abuse, we strengthen that wall.

One day we wake up and find the wall has become a fortress. We may feel relieved to have this fortification to retreat to, should there be any future attack or threat of an emotional war. But this is a maladaptive strategy, a coping mechanism that helps us survive an environment that is unsafe and out of alignment, not a way to open ourselves to the love and life we truly deserve.

As we get older, we become increasingly exiled from our heart, barred from the full expression of our joy, creativity, curiosity and wonder. We are weary prisoners who long for freedom but are cynical, suspicious and untrusting of it. Underneath the mask and many layers of personality that we've built up over the years to protect ourselves, we just don't believe that things will work out. We're alienated from hope, trust and the slipstream of faith. Often, our faith in the world has been shattered at a very deep level.

We can't 'think' faith into being, it's a felt sense in the body. Hope is the same. The intellect can't really deliver on it. You're either feeling it or you're not. The body never lies.

It takes time to trust, and it takes time to nurture a true commitment to ourselves. This is a direct result of being let down and betrayed and not believing we are worthy of that commitment. But even by reading another page of this book, you're in the process of making that commitment to yourself and building trust.

It's time to dismantle the fortress.

To help you through this process, I'll be introducing you to six emotional resourcing tools over the next couple of chapters that you can use, either alone or in combination, to self-regulate, self-soothe and ground your energy. Use them as you move deeper into your emotional heart, and in your daily life at any time. Create the habit of regularly taking a breath to check in with how you're feeling.

Always set your own pace and notice when you might need to be more generous with yourself, either in word or action. When we give ourselves the time and space for emotional resourcing, we grow what I call our 'compassionate adult'. More on this in the next chapter; for now, know that *this is self-care in action*. You're learning how to reparent yourself throughout this process. This is a medicine in itself.

•••

So, let's begin where we always begin... by bringing our awareness to our heart...

Take your journal, a pen and a warm drink, if you would like one, and settle into a quiet, comfortable space.

Close your eyes and place both hands flat on your spiritual heart in the middle of your chest.

Imagine you are sitting in a forest or a jungle under a green canopy. Trace the green leaves illuminated by the sunlight with your heart-mind and breathe in the healing vibration of this nourishing crystalline green light energy.

Breathe in for a count of four, hold your breath for a count of two and then release the breath through your mouth for a count of eight.

Continue breathing this way, becoming conscious of relaxing any tension you are holding in your shoulders and neck. Feel your back muscles loosen and melt with each breath you take.

Also, focus on breathing from your belly. This stimulates your vagus nerve, which is part of your body's 'rest and digest' parasympathetic nervous system.

Focusing on this rhythmic breathing slows down your heartbeat, stabilizes your blood pressure and sends a message to your brain to move into a calm state of mind.

Take a moment to feel the sensation of one hand covering the other one and visualize your spiritual heart underneath both hands.

Tap your heart with one finger, then two, then four, to physically connect with your chest and bring yourself back into your felt-sense body.

Showing Up for the Emotional Heart

We all have challenges to resolve, base metal to turn into gold. We've all had our emotional heart broken, silenced or forgotten at some time, and now it's time to go back to this chamber together.

Often the first time I see a client, a type of system override happens. The emotional heart is so relieved that it's finally found a safe place to rest and unburden itself of what it's been stoically carrying for such a long time that the tears will just begin to flow.

'I'm so sorry,' the client will say nervously, or 'I wasn't expecting that,' or 'Does this always happen?'

I respond with the glass bottle analogy, a simple little story, but one that I've found to be quite helpful in these instances...

Imagine you're carrying a large glass bottle. A cork has been pressed firmly into the top of this bottle and it's filled to the brim with liquid. You're holding it tightly to your chest, because you're terrified that it could slip through your fingers and smash into thousands of pieces. You feel anxious, but don't know why, because you've been carrying this bottle for so long that you've forgotten you're carrying it.

Today the invitation is to stop, remember the bottle, uncork it and pour some of the energy away.

It's safe to put the bottle down.

It's cathartic to pierce the wall that has calcified around our heart over time and profoundly transformational to surrender the stories, memories and tears that have been trapped within us for so long.

Through this process you will release old feelings that have weighed you down and impacted your joy and ability to evolve. You will transmute the blocks that have kept you in a stuck and stagnant state, quieten your negative self-talk and heal your deepest wounds. You'll wake up one morning and there'll be no bottle, just an irrepressibly joyful lightness of being...

•••

Do we all need to do this? In a recent workshop I facilitated, one of the participants was genuinely baffled by the concept that she could possess something even remotely resembling a Shadow. Her life appeared to be so 'together'. She was happily married with two healthy children. Her husband had a great job and she had a successful career. Not only had she ticked many of the boxes society expects us to tick, but she was also extremely kind and affable to her friends and everyone she met. People 'liked' her; she was a 'good' person. The suggestion of a dark side felt confusing and uncomfortable to her.

This is a response that I encounter regularly in my work. It's tough for the ego to contemplate the existence of a Shadow self, especially when our cultural or religious conditioning has told us from an early age that we're only worthy if we're good. Which translates as: 'Good = lovable; anything that isn't good = unlovable.' The idea that we could be unlovable speaks to our worst fears and creates deep anxiety and stress inside us.

> Even at a safe distance, I feared that something I said would be misinterpreted, that I would be judged harshly and cut off without warning. I was constantly worried about saying the wrong thing or offending someone. I believed that any imperfection, in my speech in particular, would make me unacceptable to others and unlovable. Living like this was a constant stress on my mind and body and made me feel disconnected from my soul power.
>
> Will

The emotional heart is like a glass bottle – often full to capacity and in desperate need of emptying. When you begin to acknowledge and process your feelings, you start to empty that bottle so it's easier to carry. This is a radical gesture of self-love.

Who wants to live like this? And it's only through alchemizing what we're carrying in the dark recesses of our Shadow that we can return to wholeness and embody our True Essence.

You don't happen to be the one soul out of the 8 billion of us currently incarnated on the planet who gets to side-step the Shadowlands. The darkness inside you is real, too, and it's time to shine a light on it.

> *'Until you make the unconscious conscious, it will*
> *direct your life, and you will call it fate.'*
> CARL JUNG

Healing Is a Choice

I returned to London from California with my three-year old son and his father. The cracks were already beginning to appear in our marriage, but I was choosing to ignore them. I was desperately trying to patch things up and skim over the painful truth that I had recreated my childhood experience in my adult relationship.

When we turn our back on the truth, we turn our back on ourselves too. This is a self-abandoning behaviour and happens when we don't love ourselves enough.

The truth was that my marriage was co-dependent and emotionally avoidant instead of intimate, present and nurturing. I could be self-reliant to the point of hyper-independent, which is a coping mechanism that makes it feel impossible to ask for help, and I'd also assumed the role of emotional caretaker in the marriage, repeating a pattern from my childhood. These were all symptoms of what educator and lecturer Pia Melody calls 'love addiction'. Love addiction and love avoidance are two sides of the same coin and we can trace the origins of all addictions, from drugs, alcohol and sex to food, gambling and shopping, to the trauma and emotional neglect and rejection we experienced in our early years.

I was clearly caught in a love-addicted relationship loop that had been stuck on repeat for my entire twenties. This persistent cycle was high-octane and intense. It consisted mainly of being in love with the idea of love. I was addicted to the whirlwind of the honeymoon phase. This felt like love but was just filling an emotional deficit within me with highs, lows and lots of drama. I was completely terrified of true intimacy, and my marriage was mirroring my avoidance issues and colluding with my intrinsic beliefs about romantic relationships. Deep down in my unconscious I believed they were untrustworthy, inconsistent and would eventually lead to abandonment and betrayal.

Healing is a choice, and one morning I woke up and decided to take responsibility for the story that I was manifesting. It was time to rewrite the narrative and rewire the unconscious emotions that lay at the root of all my conscious thoughts and subsequent reality. It was time to take the power back.

Around this time, as well as continuing the hands-on energy sessions I'd been doing in California, I started offering tarot readings at a little esoteric shop in Chelsea. It was ideal training for me, and wonderful to be of service in this way. My mother had introduced me to the tarot when I was very young and the gift of second sight had been handed down to us through her maternal line. I was honing and developing a skill that I'd possessed all my life and which fate had determined I would start to use properly.

The minute I set the clear intention to take responsibility for my own life, Spirit began to teach me, through my psychic work, how to break habitual patterns and loops. I was also guided to help people develop their own observer or wise mind. This is a tool that helps us navigate the Shadowlands and cultivate a lasting state of inner serenity.

'The root of suffering is attachment.'
BUDDHA

Growing our inner observer gives us the ability to witness and notice our thoughts and emotions without attaching to them, which means we learn to rise above them. Eventually they just wash over us. Practising non-attachment also helps us heal our past without over-identifying with it.

Before I started a reading, in the same way as when I did a hands-on energy session, I'd ask my client what they believed in. It wasn't essential that they had a strong belief in God, they just needed to be open to the power of *love*.

There wasn't one person who couldn't get their head around that possibility. And so each reading would begin with a heart opening and attunement. The spiritual heart was the sacred container and ensured that all the psychic information I received from the client's higher self and their family in the light was protected and channelled for the highest good.

What rapidly began to emerge through these sessions was how many of us are repeating patterns – painful cycles of everything from poverty and scarcity to chronic self-loathing and low self-esteem. And, as I could see only too clearly, being caught on this karmic wheel of suffering compromises our ability to successfully manifest our dreams, desires and purpose during this incarnation.

Here's a perfect example of how this can play out.

A young girl came to see me, and as she walked into the room, I almost immediately got flashes of physical violence around her.

She later confirmed that she was in an abusive relationship with her boyfriend and was incredibly unhappy but couldn't seem to find the strength to tell anyone what was happening to her or ask for help.

In that session she was able to find some strength and gain some clarity, and six months later she returned, seemingly upbeat.

'I've split up with the guy, Estelle,' she announced, smiling.

'That's great news,' I replied, not quite sure why I didn't feel we were out of the woods yet. Instead of elation, I felt apprehension, coupled with a sense of foreboding rising through my body. I started to tune in to her energy and was told by her guides that she was still at risk.

It turned out she had a new boyfriend who wasn't physically abusive to her but was verbally abusive instead. She had replaced one abusive situation with another one. She was still making choices and co-creating her reality from the limiting beliefs that she had about herself. These negative beliefs were tucked away in her unconscious.

Time and time again, I would see fabulous potential and opportunity in my clients' futures, but if they hadn't started their inner alchemical work, they wouldn't get to them. You can replace the backdrop, job or partner, but I guarantee you'll wind up with the same lived experience if nothing has transformed for you on the inside.

To help with this, I was guided to interpret the last card of the tarot spread as either the 'outcome' or the 'challenge'. I was being shown how to help my clients understand the importance of the emotional heart and the Shadow on the healing journey.

So, I'd read the overall situation as the outcome, but also start to analyse the energetic blocks as the challenge. I'd receive a precise psychic dossier about the blocks, and the stories and trauma that had created them, either in this life or other lives. This really helped bring my awareness to the specific area of healing that was needed at the time.

For example, I'd be in the middle of talking to someone about a present-day situation, when out of the darkness their hushed, soundless younger self would appear with their unacknowledged story – the unexplored story of their past that was creating their future.

These years spent in the little esoteric shop were laying the foundations for how Spirit would work through me in the future.

The House

When I'm working with someone to help them meet their Shadow and heal their emotional heart, Spirit often drops in the visual of a house.

This house is laid out in the normal way: the front door leads to various rooms on the ground floor and stairs lead up to a first floor, with more rooms and possibly an attic, while other stairs go down to the basement.

In the blink of an eye, this image offers me a simple and very effective understanding of how a person is currently showing up in their life. How? Because the house represents the way we choose to interact with life in this dimension.

Clients occupy different parts of this house, depending on how they feel about themselves at a deep cellular level. Some have a front room and kitchen area that appear to be in full working order, super-sparkly and perfect for entertaining, but they've decided that the upstairs area is off-limits. Others venture into more of who they are and might occupy a couple of the bedrooms.

I find that many people are still standing on their own doorstep, barred from any sense of their own home, lost and disconnected from themselves.

Close your eyes with me now and visualize this house for yourself. What does your house look like?

Walk around it if you can. Where can you go? Are you confined to one floor?

Does it feel light or dark inside your home?

Open your eyes and draw a rough sketch of your house in your journal and a stick figure to represent yourself. Don't overthink the drawing part – have fun with it.

Where are you in relation to your house?

Add any other images or words that come through to you.

Wherever you find yourself in your house, there's a high probability that there's a room that you've never visited. Or, if you have visited it, only you know about it. This is most definitely not a place where you invite others to be with you. No one is allowed to know that this room exists. Remember Pete's panic room?

At the beginning of this process, clients often say to me, 'Everything that's been locked away in there has been locked away *for a reason*. Why would I ever want to open the door?'

The very real fear of opening that door and stepping into our emotional heart space comes from the assumption that there's a dam inside us, and when this collapses, we'll be flooded by an ocean of emotion, a *tsunami* of self, and drown under a tidal wave of our own tears.

We've been told that crying is a sign of weakness, and so we're terrified of being exposed in this way. We're at war with our tears, which can result in a lifetime of suppressed emotion. Swallowing our tears or pushing them away is known as 'repressive coping' and Harvard studies have linked this strategy to a less resilient immune system, cardiovascular disease and mental health conditions, including stress, anxiety and depression.

When we allow our tears to flow, our body naturally releases endorphins, and these feel-good chemicals ease both physical and emotional pain. Our tears cleanse our systems of toxins and stress hormones. When you feel tears surfacing, notice the internal voices that look to shame you out of expressing them and speak kindly but firmly to those voices. They may be the voices of people you have known or your own ego. Affirm that from now on you are giving yourself permission to shed a tear, howl, sob, wail or weep. Choose to trust the intelligence of your emotional body and allow it to be expressed. God gave us our tears for a reason.

So, what's in the room?

The Shadow

Light cannot exist without darkness. This is a fundamental spiritual truth.

We all carry darkness. We all carry wounding. The drama really begins when our wounding remains unknown to us, so is unprocessed. Whilst it remains unprocessed, we're at the mercy of our triggers and 'unacceptable' emotions. These abandoned, discarded parts of our psyche take on a life of their own, like a stone gathers moss. They mobilize, form a backbone and become the inner demons that we silently battle or look to placate every day.

Western psychology describes the process of discarding aspects of ourselves as a splitting-off or fragmentation of the psyche. When we work energetically and through the heart, we are working more inter-dimensionally with our unconscious. In the process of manifesting our True Essence, our inner work naturally becomes more psychic, embodied and soulful. Indigenous shamanic culture describes fragmentation as soul loss, which leads to spiritual illness. The shaman's job is to facilitate an energetic retrieval of the lost soul parts for the full restoration of harmony and happiness.

This is how I also approach Shadow work, and we will journey to the Shadowlands with this dimension of shamanic understanding and wisdom.

The Shadow is something I'd learned about through various work I'd done in the past, but the weekend with Estelle was truly transformational... a new level of being seen fully for who I am, the light and the shadow, the parts I've desperately tried to hide and deny for most of my life...

This experience brought a newfound understanding of the importance of bringing my Shadow into the light, where it can be seen. I feel as though I've shed a lifetime of grief in the space of a couple of days...

I know in my heart the Shadow work I did with Estelle will have a profound impact on how I show up in the world from this point on, helping me to see

the world with greater clarity, without projection, and allowing me to live
with less fear and be more in my heart.

Sam

Through this process, you will begin the precious work of unlocking the untapped power of the healer, shaman and alchemist within you. We all have the power to change our own lives and you are more powerful than you can possibly imagine.

> *'YOU, ME, WE*
> *carry the Divine Spark of*
> *Creation and Wholeness*
> *within us.'*

When we make the choice to embody our healing process rather than deny it or keep it in the area of the mind, we can, however, feel apprehensive and fearful. This is a completely natural response to stepping into the unknown. Greet your fear with a loving smile and surround it with a cloak of compassion. You're learning to trust the power of your own light.

As we explore the Shadowlands, you'll meet the abandoned aspects of yourself and come to realize that they're definitely *not* the enemy. They don't get to hold you to ransom any more. Those days are done. From now on, your practice will be to meet all of who you are with compassion and love.

The Divine Feminine quality of compassion is already growing within you. It's the tenderness of your compassion that will ultimately help you invite these forsaken parts of yourself back into your heart with a newly discovered gentle grace. You'll finally be released from the torment that occurs when they remain unmet within you.

Prior to working with Estelle, I was completely unaware of my Shadow and the extent to which it was sabotaging my life – my relationships with others, but most importantly, my relationship with myself. Looking back, almost every interaction I had with another person or every approach to a challenge in my life was fuelled by destructive subconscious beliefs, the most pervasive of which was that the universe, the world that I lived in and the people in it wanted to punish and destroy me and make life as difficult as possible for me. I felt I constantly needed to be on watch and prepared for the worst. I was suspicious of everyone and everything.

Through heart-led dream analysis and inner child work, I realized that I was projecting the relationship I had with my father onto my relationship with the Divine and everyone else I was in a relationship with.

Will

Will believed that no one had his back or would meet his needs. He had also lost his authentic voice through the experience of being neglected by his father, so was unable to put his needs into words. This unexpressed disappointment and sadness had turned into impotent rage and festering resentment. Will's whole story was hidden in the Shadowlands, but would show up in his life as insidious projections that he would fire indiscriminately at the people around him. When we avoid going inwards and healing, our suffering intensifies, because our wounds are neglected and become toxic for us and everyone else in our lives. Our unprocessed Shadow tightens its grip on us.

All these elements conspired to separate Will from his heart and the power of unconditional love.

•••

It might be useful to reimagine the Shadow as baggage – it could be a large trunk or a suitcase. Remember the lower decks of our ship? Over the course of our life, all sorts of stuff has been packed away into this suitcase – fear, anger, sadness, shame, our inner child and internalized dysfunctional patterns from parents, caregivers and our school environment.

But you'll find some positive qualities locked away in the suitcase too. These can be aspects of your sexuality, sensuality, ambition, creativity, playfulness, wild nature or the parts of you that were judged as unacceptable by your family and community. Whatever they are, whilst they remain unacknowledged, like Will, you will just unwittingly project many of them onto others.

Owning Our Projections

What do we project onto others and what has been projected onto us? Becoming aware of both our internal and external projections frees us from them.

We have both negative and positive internal projections. Our negative projections are things we judge others for that we don't like about ourselves, whilst our positive projections are qualities that we have disconnected from or covet but our low self-worth would have us believe we could never embody.

We are also often subject to external projections from our families. One sibling is 'the academic one', whilst the other is 'sporty', 'handsome' or 'pretty'. I frequently see cases where parents or caregivers have a negative body image and have projected their disordered eating and critical obsession onto their child by policing their intake of food or constantly focusing on their weight, shape or size. The adult's neurosis is handed down to the child and takes root in the unconscious.

Sit for a moment and write a list of the names of everyone in your immediate circle. Include your partner, friends, boss and colleagues at work. Then add the names of other people that you might meet during the course of your week. These could be anyone from your therapist to your personal trainer or your children's schoolteacher.

What characteristics do you admire or find challenging about them? Write these traits down next to their names and consider your judgements and reactions to them.

Here are a few suggestions to assist with your self-reflection:

~ Is there a friend or a colleague at work that you find annoying because they're too loud or outspoken?

~ Do you judge people? Do you assume some sort of superiority or view some people as the enemy? Consider whether they are holding up a mirror to you, reflecting what remains disowned in your Shadow.

~ Do you relate to Will's story and find yourself constantly second-guessing or overly suspicious of your partner or friends with no evidence to back up that feeling? Is this based on a belief that you'll eventually be abandoned by the person you love because you were emotionally abandoned by one or both parents?

~ Are you in awe of a friend's power, wit, intelligence, confidence, fitness level, luck, beauty, style, success or drive and put them on a pedestal or hide behind them? These are qualities that you might long to possess but believe are completely out of your reach. If you don't do the work to access and express these qualities in yourself, at some point you'll feel envious or resentful of those who do. You could even end up secretly hating them for what they have.

All these feelings may be unconscious, but they'll still be simmering away and impacting your ability to call in your dreams and co-create your future. Think back to standing at the window, transmitting your unique radio show to the universe. When the Shadow is unprocessed, it's super-murky. It lowers your frequency and really messes with your innate magic and power to manifest.

But if you take ownership of these parts of yourself and bring them into the light, they transform and your energy aligns. You alchemize your trauma, and your positive projections can dynamically inspire and motivate you instead of fuelling negative emotions that disable and undermine you. You become a pure channel for quantum healing, miracles and abundance.

A simple example of this was a client, let's call her Kate, who came to see me with low-level depression and anxiety. Married for over 20 years, with children who were about to leave the nest to go off to college, she had already identified that her current mood was connected to an overriding feeling of no longer having a purpose.

Having been defined by motherhood, Kate found her self-esteem at an all-time low. She had left her career over a decade before and couldn't see a way back into the world of work.

We spent some time meeting the notion that she lacked direction and discovered that she'd actually been falling in love with yoga and meditation over the course of a few years. She really looked up to her yoga teacher but didn't feel clever or 'spiritual' enough to even ask her where she had done her yoga teacher training.

Kate was disconnected from this new passion because she felt like an imposter, fearful, self-conscious and out of her league. She couldn't possibly imagine herself studying or teaching it. She responded with embarrassment and shame when I suggested that perhaps at this stage in her life she was being called to be of service in a different way and step into her power.

Over a couple of sessions, we worked on the fear that Kate was holding in the Shadow around her intelligence, being seen and assuming a role of authority in the community. I reminded her that our brief time here on the planet is an adventure. That it is about following the signs and trusting what makes your heart sing.

And Kate did just that. She freed herself from her limiting beliefs, threw caution to the wind and, at 50, travelled for the first time to India, where she completed a yoga teacher-training course. Now she feels alive again.

Wake-Up Call or Crisis?

'There came a time when the risk to remain tight in the bud
was more painful than the risk it took to blossom.'
ANAÏS NIN

There's a moment when your soul will look to wake you from your slumber, so that you begin your emotional heart-healing and return to all that you are. This date with destiny will kick-start your healing journey.

That might sound wonderful on the surface, but the wake-up call usually takes the form of a crisis. It's often a dark night of the soul and yet our breakdowns are blessings in disguise...

I was a super-successful choreographer, working all over the world in fashion and music, and yet I felt depressed, lost, confused and disconnected. Nothing was making sense, life on this planet felt heavy and empty, there were so many questions going through my mind every single day.

'Why am I here?' 'Why are we here?' 'What do I want from this life?' 'What is my purpose?' Big questions that I'd never asked myself before. It felt like my soul wasn't in my body any more and I was on a mission to find it again.

Pat

Have you experienced a dark night of the soul? Or a few of them? The dark night was first described in a poem by 16th-century priest and mystic St John of the Cross. It's a time of existential crisis when a soul finds itself in a constant state of questioning, malaise and despair. It heralds an ego-death and subsequent awakening. When you find yourself in the middle of one, buckle up, it's sure to be one helluva ride, but these dark nights crack us open and keep us on our evolutionary spiritual path.

In these moments, we're standing at a crossroads. One road leads us back to all that we already know. It's brightly lit and guarantees a swift return to the welcoming arms of the limiting stories that cause us so much suffering but are oddly homely and familiar.

And the other road? The other road is wholly unknown to us, unfamiliar in every way. And yet there's something inexplicable beckoning us forward – a faint whisper here, a murmur on the wind that we think we may have heard... Was it a whisper of encouragement or just a hollow echo reverberating around the abyss that lies before us?

In the beginning, that whisper will come and go. But it will grow stronger day by day. Those murmurings are our own soul calling us home.

Imagine a lighthouse beam on a dark winter's night in the middle of a storm. We are out at sea in zero visibility, battling dark waves in a little boat. We're holding on for dear life, with white knuckles and numb fingers, and then we see a light – faint at first, but on the horizon nonetheless. We're not alone, after all.

When 'the dark night of the soul' comes knocking on your heart's door, you're often guided to a healer, and I feel blessed I was guided to the warm, lovely Estelle Bingham... but I went in complete resistance, as I wasn't going to allow her to dismantle any of the stories I held sacred around the subject of 'love'.

I don't think I even had the language back then to understand what was going on... nor did I have the self-love to admit to myself what was actually absent from myself and from my whole life. Back then I was so confused and scared... yet I knew I needed... to be guided back to love.

The first few sessions we talked about love, mainly the kind of 'love' I put on a pedestal. We talked about my mom, my dad, my brothers and my sisters, my exes, and I didn't even realize I was speaking with undeniable conviction about why they deserved to be on that pedestal. I was fully unaware of how I had learned to gaslight my own emotions around the experiences I had of neglect, hurt and deceit.

Session after session, Estelle guided me to an understanding of why I allowed a kind of 'love' that actually was infused with hurt and harm. Session after session, we healed all the energetic scar tissue that I had built around my heart, because of a lifetime of survival mechanisms from my conditioned ego-mind.

With her guidance, I learned to see through many of the illusions I was holding around what I thought 'love' should be and feel like. I learned to see that I was repeating a kind of 'love' that wasn't serving me in order to feel a sense of belonging and connection. I learned to see that I was worthy of so much more. I'm now learning to hold that beautiful kind of pure love, both for myself and for others in my life.

Will

'However long the night, the dawn will break...'
AFRICAN PROVERB

There is so much abundance waiting for you right now. It's got your name written all over it, but until you decide to value yourself, you'll still be out at sea.

Finding a safe harbour is about feeling safe in the world and safe in the body. That's our birthright. But so many of us don't feel safe in our body, and because of that we don't feel we belong, which means that we don't feel we can really connect with others. They feel separate and different from us. But ultimately, we're just afraid of getting hurt.

Everyone has the opportunity to find a safe harbour during this incarnation. It's what we were born to do. And that safe place already exists within us, in our heart. When we anchor into our spiritual heart, our full range of emotions can begin to flow properly.

Having a safe space to voice [my] rage, without fear of judgement, has helped me be more accepting of myself and let go of the need to be a 'good person' with no negative emotions. I realize that I need to feel and express a certain amount of anger to keep myself safe in relationship with others and that it is time to bring this out of the Shadow and use it in my day-to-day life. I have learned that this is called 'sacred anger'. I no longer judge myself as much for feeling angry and realize the value of anger in my life. I feel I am living more and more as a whole person with a whole range of emotions.

Will

Follow the light, however faint.
Follow that flicker. It's the seed
of hope growing inside you.

Embodying our sacred anger is vital for clearing our throat chakra and is one of the ways we can find our voice. When we're connected to our voice, we begin to speak our truth and create new boundaries. Saying, 'I don't like that,' 'That's not for me,' or just a simple 'no' is essential to feeling truly safe in our body and in the world.

Having boundaries actually helps us become more vulnerable in relationships, because we're not afraid to maintain a healthy energetic line in the sand where I end and you begin. This line doesn't mean I love you any less, it just means I love myself too, and this means we're choosing not to merge or lose ourselves in others.

When we're anchored in our heart, we feel safe enough to risk loving with all of who we are. We're prepared to put ourselves on the line, because we know that when we can hold ourselves safe, then we can lean into intimacy more. We can learn to trust love.

•••

So, let's deepen our exploration of the Shadowlands now. The most important thing to know in this moment is that you won't get lost in the dark. You're completely safe. Everything you're about to see in the darkness is you.

Settle into a comfortable space, either sitting or lying down. Play some relaxing music (639Hz Solfeggio frequency if possible), place your hands on your heart, close your eyes and take some long, deep breaths to bring yourself into heart awareness and the present moment.

Imagine a beautiful crystalline blue energy pouring down through the top of your crown, through your throat and filling your heart. This light forms the shape of a beautiful blue flame that expands with each breath you take. This is the light that you will take with you into the darkness.

You are standing at the top of a spiral staircase. The area is very well lit with bright torches. Begin to descend.

At the bottom of this staircase, you find yourself standing in front of an ancient wooden door. We are entering the Shadowlands.

Announce silently to your unconscious that you have arrived here with no judgement and that you are open to meeting and integrating all aspects of your fractured self.

Turn the handle of the heavy door and step over the threshold.

As you step into the darkness, feel the beautiful bright light of the blue flame that is glowing in your heart expand and grow warm within your chest. This flame lights the way for you.

You're in a long corridor with rooms on either side. Most of the doors have notices on them: a theme and a corresponding line of negative self-talk that you may recognize.

Read these as you walk along the corridor and allow your intuition to guide you to the Shadow aspect that you'd like to start with first...

~ You're not good enough – 'I'm too broken to ever heal/Nothing ever changes in my life.'

~ You don't *deserve* abundance – 'I don't attract money, opportunities or love.'

~ Your *dreams* will never come true – 'Nothing ever works out for me/I've been left behind by life/It's too late for me.'

~ You don't *belong* here – 'No one likes or understands me/I'm so alone/I can't find my tribe.'

~ You're *too* fat/thin/ugly/stupid/intelligent/young/old/poor/wealthy... – 'I'm too fat/thin/ugly, etc.'

~ The *universe doesn't have your back* – 'The universe/God has let me down/betrayed me/Other people get all the luck in life. I can never catch a break.'

~ You need to be *perfect* – 'If it's not perfect, it's not good enough/I need to be top of the class/scrutinize everything I do.'

~ You need to be in *control* – 'I'm out of control/I need to know what's coming next/I don't feel safe unless I'm in control/Everything will fall apart without me/I'm responsible for other people's happiness.'

~ It's not *safe* to be in your body – 'I'm out of my body most of the time/I'm ashamed to own my sexuality/sensuality/sexual needs/fantasies.'

~ You're not *seen or heard* – 'No one ever listens to me/My opinions are worthless/I'm a burden/I'm afraid to take up space.'

~ You're an *imposter*/You're inferior/less than – 'I'm going to be found out/I'm not who people think I am/Someone can take my place.'

~ You don't *deserve* success – 'I'm afraid to take the first step or any risks because I'll fail/success will overwhelm me.'

~ You're a *failure* – 'I've failed so many times/I always get things wrong/I never win at anything.'

Each room has its own story, voice and wisdom. Go to the Shadow aspect you have decided to start with and imagine yourself opening the door and sitting down on a chair in the middle of the room.

Notice if there is anything or anyone else in this space. Ask your unconscious, 'Why do I feel like this? Where does this belief/feeling originate from? Who spoke these words to me when I was growing up? Why have I repressed these feelings? How old do I feel in this moment? Do you have any other messages for me?'

Give your Shadow time to speak to you. A scene, memory or person may drop into your awareness. Perhaps one or more emotions will bubble up from the underworld of your subconscious. Embrace whatever arrives.

Visualize the flame inside your heart beaming a luminous light into each corner of the room, warmly and lovingly dissolving the darkness here.

Journal Prompts

* Journal about what has emerged, including the exact words that you heard during the meditation. Some of these words form the basis of your negative self-talk.

* Turn the negative self-talk into a positive affirmation. So, 'You have to be perfect; if you're not perfect, you're not lovable' becomes 'I give myself permission to be perfectly imperfect. I give myself permission to be human. I *am* love.'

* Repeat your affirmation to yourself when you hear the voice of the Shadow aspect pop into your awareness at any point in your day. Make this part of your daily practice.

As you explore the Shadowlands, you'll add other Shadow aspects to this list that are personal to you. You'll also be recovering your inner child and exploring shame more intimately in the next couple of chapters.

I'll be with you, but you really get to set the pace with this work, so you can continue reading through to the end of the book whilst still exploring and returning to different rooms and corners of your emotional heart. Give yourself time.

Be patient and gentle with yourself. What's important is that you've made the choice to heal and right here, right now, you're in the process of manifesting your True Essence. This is the greatest commitment to yourself that you've ever made.

Take Time to Trust

Although the journey back to wholeness is a precious thing of beauty, miracles and magic, it is never linear, so don't be too surprised if you wake up feeling as if you're back at square one a few times during this process. The healing journey will ebb and flow like the tides. One day you can have a massive breakthrough and the next week something or someone can blow you way off course and many of your old anxieties and fears reappear to wreak havoc with your peace.

You might think you're being tested by the universe. An old wound that you believed was healed or healing may burst open again, and you're suddenly fully triggered, acting out and responding with all your old coping strategies.

But the time you spend detouring is invaluable. When you find yourself back in a familiar situation, you're being invited to embody what you've healed or are healing in the real world in real time. It's a perfect opportunity to truly embody and integrate what you're learning.

When this happens, take more time to trust and nourish your commitment to yourself. Use one of the self-regulation practices (see pages 36, 74, 115, 143, 186, 224) and this affirmation:

*'I see, witness, notice you, but I am not you. I acknowledge
that you are a result of my abandonment/scarcity/
ancestral/sexual [as applicable] wound and I surround
you with the cloak of compassion and let you go.'*

Remember there is a way to alchemize what you hold in your Shadow. And, as Rosie reminds us, however difficult, it's well worth it:

Healing is not for the faint-hearted. It's not daffodils and butterflies and lovely-smelling incense, or, as Estelle said to me once at a retreat, 'This isn't the Disney World of healing, Rosie. This is the real deal. What happened to you as a child was vicious and life-threatening. So, at times, healing is going to feel like that too.'

These vicious and life-threatening experiences had happened to me over 30 years before, but my heart and mind held on to them until I was strong enough to hold them and face them myself. And, eventually, let them pass through me.

Estelle held these experiences up for me, and held me up while I confronted them, one by one. Gradually, we healed layer after layer, shedding those skins of darkness, trauma and stuck pain... I went into the darkest of places within myself, and Estelle held my hand and the torch. Shining it into every dark corner. But only when I was ready to see what was there.

I felt like I was walking through a dark labyrinth where sometimes I couldn't see a way out and it felt never-ending. I was walking through my personal dark night of the soul...

But we turned that corner together and carried on until every last bit of pain was dug up, pulled out and turned into wisdom. I awakened to self-love and self-nurturing.

Finally, I have my personal dignity and the freedom to build the life that I deserve and that will make me truly happy.

Rosie

> 'The secret to happiness is freedom... and the
> secret to freedom is courage.'
> THUCYDIDES

Take a moment to acknowledge your courage and how far you've come.

Journal Prompts

* Think about your past and reflect on how you've survived in the face of difficult situations and adversity.

* Write down your age, the experience(s) and then the words: 'I celebrate you. I'm so proud of you. I honour your courage.'

You might be celebrating getting out of bed today. It's enough. Be proud of yourself.

You're doing great...

A Radical Act of Self-Love

The key to wholeness is not rejecting the Shadow parts of yourself, however unacceptable they may appear, but acknowledging them, loving them, and so integrating and alchemizing them.

As psychologist James Hillman says in *Meeting the Shadow*,

> *'How much charity and compassion have we for our own weakness and sickness?... Loving oneself is no easy matter, just because it means loving all of oneself, including the shadow where one is inferior and socially so unacceptable.'*

This process may not be easy, but it will help to remember that divinity also exists within you. Within us all. We're predictable like that.

We're all unique beings, endowed with beautiful gifts, and it's our birthright to discover and manifest those gifts. These specific talents can only express themselves though us individually. *And* we're part of the whole, connected to all things, both animate and non-animate. We're connected to all of Creation.

So, whatever has happened to you, remember you are worthy of love – in fact, a radical act of self-love.

> *'Our hearts have all been broken,*
> *silenced or forgotten at some time.*
> *Our hearts carry so much for us...*
> *often in darkness.*
> *When we create space,*
> *somewhere...*

to be with our heart,
to listen – listening at the door of self...
to all that our heart has witnessed so far,
we are companioning our heart.
This is a very special moment in our lifetime.
We begin to build the harbour,
the safe place for the return –
return to self, return to love.'

Shining a light on all that your emotional heart has been carrying for you is a radical act of self-love.

Then you will understand the true meaning of companionship.

You will understand what it means *to companion yourself.*

To befriend and cheerlead yourself.

To be the rock that you dream of finding in another person.

It's a moment in time when you realize that there's a whole lot more to you than you had previously imagined.

I can definitely guarantee that the day will come when you wake up in the morning and feel deeply grateful for this moment in time.

So, you have everything you need right now to feel safe in your body and experience the feeling of belonging.

We are bound by the imagined constraints of time and space in this dimension, but they are an illusion. This is not to ignore that the older we get, the more difficult it can become to transform, because our sense of who we are becomes more entrenched. But you can step onto that road back to your True Essence at any age. All that's needed is a willingness to step onto your own road back home and transform your life, as Adrianna discovered:

I had a lifelong series of disastrous relationships, some very long, some short, some even simultaneous, and had vowed to take myself 'off the road', as my choices were essentially re-enactments of all the chaos and trauma I'd grown up with. I would confuse familiarity with comfort. I admitted I had no idea how to find what I was looking for and decided to be celibate until I found that someone.

From 45 to 60 I lived in the same house, attended 12-step meetings very regularly, had a wonderful dog, made new friends and solidified some old friendships. I was undergoing quite intense psychotherapy all this time. Then my dog died, I turned 60 and I decided to downsize, but to my astonishment, I was headhunted to work in the USA. I took the job and relocated in 2013. I felt a fresh start would be a great idea and even possibly offer the chance of meeting someone.

Instead, I entered probably the loneliest period of my life. The work was incredibly hard – 12-hour days, on call 24/7, very heavy caseloads and learning new methods and protocols with no one taking time to help me...

I eventually turned things around and implemented several changes at work, while digging very deep and finding a real sense of self. I figured this would prepare me to spend my old age alone.

I returned to London in 2018... re-engaged with old friends and gradually picked up my life. I kept on weekly sessions with the trauma therapist I'd been seeing in the US. Then Covid hit. I spent the first six months entirely alone, not seeing anyone I knew. While this felt incredibly familiar, something clicked and I thought, Ah, I really need to do something. So, in 2021, at the age of 69, I went on a dating site. What else could I do in lockdown? Eventually, after many, many false starts and a few horrors, I clicked with a man who lived in another country. He was Buddhist, almost a monk, and claimed he wasn't looking for a relationship, but was lonely too. Our correspondence was lengthy and deep.

Now I realize my foray into dating wasn't as much about the men I might find as it was about myself and healing a part of myself that had been hidden for so long but was still alive and full of longing.

A friend had been talking of the 'Love Retreat' that she'd attended and, while feeling highly sceptical, nonetheless I had observed this friend really blossom, so I decided to give it a go.

Almost straight away on meeting Estelle I felt warm and at home. It was astonishing, a very deep process, one of the most profound experiences of my life, and in healing an immense, life-altering trauma that had occurred when I was 24, I realized I was pouring all my longing and loneliness into an incredibly safe cul-de-sac, i.e. a monk-like man on another continent. With Estelle's help, I decided to somehow pull back all this energy and channel it towards someone who could meet it, and perhaps more importantly, meet me!

If you know Estelle, you won't be surprised by this next part. Within 24 hours of leaving the Love Retreat, I was contacted by someone on the same site as the 'monk'. We talked, texted and Zoomed for almost three weeks before we met. I have been seeing him now for over two years. It has its complications, as most relationships do, and I am considerably older, but I have never felt so alive, and so full of joy, as I do now.

Adrianna

You, too, have chosen to take a step forward and shine a light into the dark corners of your emotional heart. What now? How will you choose to transform and transmute a negative experience of love into a positive one?

Know that the Earth plane responds to the universal laws like a well-oiled cosmic machine. The souls that move into and out of our life bring us both good and bad medicine. Teachers, friends, bullies, work colleagues, bosses, lovers, partners, boyfriends, girlfriends, husbands, wives and children don't just miraculously happen to us! They all form an intrinsic part of our reawakening to love.

The bottom line is that even if our formative relationships with parents or siblings have had a negative effect on our development, these people were most certainly in our life in order to deepen our relationship with love and to remind us of our true nature.

We'll continue our exploration of the Shadowlands by looking at what happens when we're children, how we get more separated from our True Essence as a result of our experiences and how we can now bring compassion to our inner child and continue this journey back to wholeness.

Know that you're travelling a holy path back to Love.

CHAPTER 5

The Hidden Child

'Childhood tiptoed out.
Silence slid in like a bolt.'
ARUNDHATI ROY

I am four or five years old. I have a black cat and a small dog called Goldie. This is 1970s Hackney in east London, one of the most underprivileged areas in the UK, a rich hotch-potch of reprobates, artists, rebels, bohemians, first-generation Caribbeans, Africans, Asians, Cypriots and real-life East Enders born within the sound of Bow bells.

As children, we all play together on our street, a raggle-taggle of ages, scrapes and bruises. My true friends are John, who is similar in age to me, the youngest of an Irish family of four siblings, and Lisa, his sister, who is one of the middle children.

I am secretly very in love with John, but can never quite muster the courage to let him know, and he appears to be completely oblivious to the feelings that have begun to blossom inside me.

Most weekends, when my mother and Reg drive out to the countryside to walk the dog, we take John and Lisa with us. Three can most definitely be a crowd, but we all love the sense of adventure and escape that we discover out of the city in nature, and we form an unlikely but intense bond for a few years.

John's father is a nice man. When he's awake, he's very smiley and loves to crack a joke. He does spend an awful lot of time lying on the floor behind the sofa in a drunken stupor, but he isn't an angry drunk. John's mum, who is a nice woman, often loses her temper with him and, desperate and in tears, shouts at his unmoving body. This happens like clockwork and has a particular rhythm all of its own.

We all have our stories.

A few doors down the street, my little feet dangle over the kitchen chair and don't yet touch the floor.

My mother brought me back here as a newborn from the Salvation Army Mothers' Hospital and bundled me into a corner of the brown leather sofa, because she didn't have enough money to buy a cot.

My father is mostly absent, but my mum spends her time with Reg, who likes metal-detecting for Roman coins, identifying birdsong when we are walking in the forest and indulging in drinking sessions with his friends.

My mum and I live in two rooms in a rambling four-storey Victorian house opposite Hackney Downs. This is a rare piece of common land in the middle of the city. Surviving from pre-medieval times, common land is owned by no one. So, there are no fences or rules or regulations here, just a wild expanse of green and an army of old London plane trees that often like to whisper their secrets to me on the wind.

Despite the poverty and chaos, my mother is a warrior, fierce and extraordinary. In between juggling my childcare, she joins an American life insurance company and within weeks becomes one of their top-performing sales negotiators. A few years later, when I'm eight years old, she will buy our house for cash. Among other things, she's a workaholic. She's doing the best she can.

At first, though, we have very little. We live hand to mouth and she's always late with the rent, but she bakes a delicious carrot cake and teaches me about the importance of magic, fairies and meditation.

And we spend hours playing everything from Carole King and the Beatles to Alice Coltrane, Nina Simone and Jefferson Airplane full blast on her record player. She claps and whoops and loves to cheer me on. I learn how to dance and stomp with pure abandon. It's truly uninhibited and lots of fun.

But each day, as I grow into myself and individuate, she becomes more overwhelmed. Or perhaps I'm just noticing it more. She's always shouting at me. Something about me being selfish, answering back or just being wrong. The house is full of tantrums and drama.

There's a profound complexity to managing an immature parent when you're growing up with them. It's a full-time job. In my case, I lived through the push–pull of the 'I hate you, don't leave me' cycle, a powerful compulsion that my mother had to reject and abandon coupled with a deep-seated fear of being abandoned herself.

Stuck in her own child-like state, the victim/child deeply resents having to parent. Instead, she is physically and verbally abusive, unpredictable, mercurial, erratic and at times very cruel. She is a wounded child attempting to parent a child, but, despite herself, wounding that child every day.

I have often said to my mother, 'Let's work this karmic stuff out, because I don't want to be born within a 50-mile radius of you next time!'

But let's get real here for a minute, My mother didn't 'just happen' upon this dysfunction. Like it fell out of the sky and landed on her head at birth! Her internal chaos was handed down to her by all of those who came before her, who were also caught in a cycle of unprocessed trauma and suffering. We all have our stories...

A survivor of, among other things, a depressed, disassociated mother and an aggressive alcoholic father, it was no great surprise that my mother was living beneath layer upon layer of stagnant pain, fully charged, very messy and extremely lethal to the touch. She learned to mother from a line of motherless mothers.

It was always destined to end in tears.

> 'A family is a place where minds come in contact with one another.
> If these minds love one another, the home will be as beautiful as
> a flower garden. But if these minds get out of harmony with one
> another, it is like a storm that plays havoc with the garden.'
> BUDDHA

It's actually my mother's rage that has the power to take me out at the knees and deals the heftiest of blows to my emotional body. There's a switch buried deep within her that I don't understand when I'm a child. When that switch flips, a feeling of absolute dread floods my entire being. Her unbridled rage is quite something to behold, let alone live through.

Her rage and emotional neglect leave me internally shattered over and over again, day in, day out.

But then, one afternoon, I just know this isn't going to last forever. I can feel angelic presence by now, and this also coincides with learning Transcendental Meditation. I probably have my first download at this time too – a powerful moment of inner knowing and guidance from my higher self.

The eagle eye perspective I gain in those moments means that my childhood doesn't have the power to completely annihilate me. (In retrospect this feels like the moment when I'm first connected to the observer within me.) I survive my mother's ever-shifting moods by avoiding them, spending hours in the garden and losing myself in the books I read. By the age of eight, I have also started writing poetry as a way of making sense of the world.

Something in my spirit says, 'Estelle, you're going to be okay.'

•••

But regardless of whether or not we're connecting with angelic frequencies or receiving the odd download, growing up with emotionally immature parents takes its toll on us. We learn how to walk on eggshells, squash our authentic voices and suppress our natural needs and wants. We also become hypervigilant and fearful around their narcissism, toxic eruptions, unpredictable moods and mental health.

The trauma that sends our inner child into hiding can range from sexual, physical or verbal abuse to having parents who were just emotion phobic. More often than not, it centres around the abandonment we felt when our parents, caregivers or other family members didn't manage to adequately meet our emotional needs. It might also be the result of an accident, surgery or illness experienced as a child, or specific events at school, like being bullied or abused by other children or teachers.

You may have been in survival mode from the very beginning of your life because of your birth experience and/or the emotions that your mother was processing during her pregnancy. Was she excited about having a baby? Was she grieving or depressed whilst she was carrying you? Was she feeling loved, safe and supported, or was she scared or ambivalent about becoming a mother?

Being exposed to harmful stress in childhood and adolescence means that the brain will spend most of its time in fight, flight, freeze or fawn mode and can get stuck there. Our systems are adrenalized and hyperalert all the time, which hugely impacts our physical and mental health and wellbeing.

We develop a false self and maladaptive coping strategies to help negotiate the faultline of emotional neglect that we're experiencing, and at what cost? *Know that there is always a cost.*

In his book *Waking the Tiger,* psychotherapist and founder of the Somatic Experiencing technique Peter Levine writes: 'Part of the dynamic of trauma is that it cuts us off from our internal experience, as a way of protecting our organisms from sensations and emotions that could be overwhelming.' He explains that our maladaptive behaviours are actually 'our safety valves... Anorexia, insomnia, promiscuity and manic hyperactivity are only a few of the symptoms that can ensue when the organism's natural functions become maladaptive.'

Abuse and trauma hardwire our brain and nervous system to respond to life in a particular way. We're more prone to PTSD, weakened immunity and habitual disassociation, and our emotions are generally more dysregulated. Sometimes we develop problems with focusing, memory and learning. Studies show that as adults we're at much greater risk of suffering from anxiety, depression and suicidal behaviour. Trauma also impacts our attachment style and ability to form enduring, loving and functioning relationships. We often have an avoidant, anxious or disorganized attachment style and need to do the inner work to learn how to attach to another person securely, with trust, care and love.

The great news is that a traumatized brain can heal. Recent discoveries in brain imaging prove what's been understood spiritually for centuries: the present moment is more powerful than the past. So, we can heal right here, right now. We all have the power to remap our brain, because we're so much more than our thoughts, and what we focus our attention on manifests as our reality. So, daily self-care, self-love routines and practices do create new neural pathways for us.

You get to choose which neural superhighway you want your brain to build for you. You have the power...

Here is a visualization to help you self-regulate and self-soothe. You can use it at any time during the True Essence Process. It's short and simple, so a perfect tool to use when you're at work, travelling or out and about socially...

The Mystic Anchor

Bring your hands into the centre of your chest and breathe deeply into your mystic heart.

Visualize slowly dropping an anchor into the calm ocean of this space within you. Notice how the water ripples for a moment as the anchor sinks to the ocean floor and then peacefully rests again.

Breathe into the stillness. Absorb the blue expanse of the sea that surrounds you and the golden light of the sky.

Drop your mystic anchor into the ocean of your heart whenever you need to connect with your inner peace.

Custodians

'If there is light in the soul, there will be beauty in the person. If there is beauty in the person, there will be harmony in the house. If there is harmony in the house, there will be order in the nation. If there is order in the nation, there will be peace in the world.'
CHINESE PROVERB

Our parents carry karmic and ancestral information and baggage of their own. And like it or not, we all choose our parents because they will help us to evolve and grow in this lifetime. They are our custodians.

Earlier, I spoke about the abyss that exists inside us when our soul arrives here and experiences separation from Spirit, or pure consciousness. This widens when our caregivers don't know how to love, or their love is toxic, conditional or transactional. But both the presence and the lack of love in childhood forces our soul into a deeper relationship with love.

'You made the decision to be here again.
Abundance, success, joy and peace are tributaries of this great energy.
Being deeply loved by someone gives you strength,
while loving someone deeply gives you courage.'
LAO TZU

As young children, we have only just left the infinite oceans of unconditional love. These oceans are what we call God, Spirit, Source or the universe. If it helps, you can imagine them as a dimension of pure consciousness or awareness. At this time, unconditional love is the only energy that we recognize. This is the frequency we compute at a cellular level. Any other vibration corrupts the original software!

We are born with the innate need to feel warm, enveloped, nurtured and safe. We yearn to be held, rocked, stroked, kissed and cuddled. We just can't get enough of it, and in those first hours, days, weeks and years we make sense of the world through the physical and emotional experience of love.

The love we receive from our parents or caregivers provides us with an invisible cord that literally grounds us into the physical plane. The psychoanalyst and paediatrician Donald Winnicott introduced the idea of 'good enough mothering', where parents don't need to be perfect, but are responsive and sympathetic enough to their child's needs to nourish this cord of secure attachment.

Our emotional circuitry is actually very simple. Imagine a roughly hewn circuit board, like one you might have seen in a school science experiment demonstrating how electricity works. There are a couple of wires sticking up in the air haphazardly, with a light bulb fixed right in the middle of the board, waiting for the big moment: the grand *fusing*! It's not difficult – wire A connects to wire B connects to wire C, and Bob's your uncle, the light bulb goes on.

This light bulb represents our ability to shine in this lifetime. It lights up our deepest desires, dreams and purpose. As children, though, we don't have the awareness or tools to hardwire ourselves. It's also not part of the job description – *parents* are the ones entrusted to connect the correct wires to one another.

Sometimes, though, one or both parents have absolutely no idea what they're doing. The wires are clumsily put together, so the bulb may go on intermittently but then switch off whenever it feels like it – the inevitable result of a loose connection!

In other cases, the circuitry might be overly complex, so the power source is compromised and the most the bulb can muster is a low-level dull beam. Sometimes the hardwiring is just downright bad. Then there's no light. Ever.

If you're reading this, some part of your spirit has chosen to rewire itself.

Emotional Retreat

Love in its purest form is straightforward. If we're not loved in a straightforward way as children, we just don't get it. We're left feeling insecure, confused and deeply disappointed. It's actually heartbreaking for us. These feelings may not be registered consciously, but they're stored in our subconscious and lay the foundations for how much love we believe we deserve later in life.

Spending time in the Shadowlands reveals how patterns are created and repeated; how what we experience, witness or internalize as a child will manifest in some way later in our life. Our personal and professional relationships mirror our childhood experience of love and relationship. It we didn't feel loved unconditionally as children, then deep down we believe we're unlovable. All our future relationships will follow a particular script until we decide to return home to ourselves.

In order to survive the great betrayal of not being loved unconditionally by our custodians, we have no choice but to become emotional survivalists. This is when we back away from our heart and abandon our inner child. The inner child becomes hidden.

For some, the shutting down of the heart is a stealth mission, a well-executed retreat to a barren emotional desert, a conscious dash for the hills. Others will just find themselves in that 'safe' emotional desert, not really conscious of how they got there, dazed, confused, but shut down all the same.

When we back away from our emotional heart, we also check out of the present. It's like pressing the eject button in a light aircraft. If we've witnessed violence, abuse or got lost in the crossfire of divorce or adult arguments, it's natural to dissociate as a way to manage the upset.

However we exit the heart, one of the most important things that we do is to make sure that we mine the surrounding area with state-of-the art emotional explosives. No one's getting back in there. We just can't risk it. 'Maim or be maimed!' is the battle cry. And we won't be maimed again.

We think we're very clever. But actually, we're very afraid. It is that simple.

By making the conscious or unconscious decision to close the door on our emotional heart, we also close the door on our inner child and the magic of our childhood, and everything that's held within that slipstream of energy. We repress our innocence, wonder, awe, trust, creativity, sense of adventure, spontaneity, playfulness and the expectation that our needs will be met.

This separation is a deviation from the path of love. We start to put on armour and lay the foundations for our fortress. Now we have deserted our heart, our vulnerability is no longer a superpower. We believe it to be a weakness.

This often leads to people completely disconnecting from the truth of their own experience, to the point of gaslighting themselves about it. I hear 'I had a great childhood' or 'I'm fine' all the time.

Sometimes we even suffer from a trauma-impacted memory, which means we're unable to recall chapters of our childhood. This type of emotional amnesia neutralizes the trauma, but is unable to resolve it.

This leaves us deeply confused as adults. We feel broken inside and are mostly preoccupied with feelings of unworthiness, shame, anger and despair. We can be chronic people-pleasers, seek to create safety through control and lack healthy boundaries. The daily management of our overriding anxiety and fear of abandonment creates a hollow emptiness inside that we look to fill with toxic behaviours, relationships or self-medication.

Otherwise, we might just be in denial. This is the most common ego-defence I see in sessions.

Retrospectively, the work that I did with Estelle made me realize that I didn't have a happy childhood in the sense of a modern upbringing and focus on mental wellbeing and a loving environment.

My parents had an arranged marriage and were of two very different temperaments; they didn't love each other then. They tolerated each other and tried to keep things going one day at a time.

Some days were a struggle – my mum would scream at us or there would be an argument that escalated into domestic violence. There was a lot of domestic violence, some aimed at me directly.

I was an introvert – not an introvert who's talkative around those they know, but an observer. I recall being an observer for most of my formative years. Observing from the corner of the classroom, observing in my seat on coach rides to swimming lessons, observing in family gatherings. I would study hard and keep my head down.

In stark contrast, my sister was the life and soul of the party. She was boisterous and loud and always seemed to be having more fun than I ever did. I always felt in her shadow, even though I was older than her by a year and a couple of months.

I would frequently wet the bed, which I was later told was trauma related, but in parallel I was an old soul trying to figure out how I had landed where I was and what was going on. Why am I here? What's the point of this? What am I here to learn? For many years I stayed quiet and pondering.

Erika

When you go into the Shadowlands in search of your inner child, you'll find them exactly where you left them all those years ago and they will tell you everything. But you'll need to let your guard down and give yourself permission to be vulnerable again to get there.

This may sound alarming, but it's only when we decide to heal as adults and journey back home to our mystic heart that there's any hope of reconciliation with this hidden child.

The retreat was the first time I had given any thought to my inner child. I had heard the term, but never connected with the concept. In many ways, I had a very happy childhood, so I didn't feel I was traumatized by the experience. I love my parents very much, and I was adamant I wasn't going to blame them for any difficulties I was having now.

But of course, it wasn't about 'blame', it was about understanding what made you who you are and how you can learn and grow from any traumas you experienced growing up. Once I realized that those on the retreat weren't judging me, my childhood or my parents, I relaxed into the process. I felt supported by my cohort and Estelle, and I could look with adult eyes at some of the experiences I had growing up and see how they had forced my inner child to take on greater responsibility than a child of that age is ready to embrace.

During the retreat, I started to peel back the layers, and over the next year I got to know my inner child better and better. What came out of that was a greater sense of autonomy in my own life. The hang-ups I had from childhood about feeling responsible for the happiness of my family are subsiding and I am better at maintaining healthy boundaries while remaining as compassionate as ever... I can speak more from the heart now; I am more aware of my own instincts.

Emma

Like Emma, so many of us unwittingly banish our inner child to the Shadowlands. It's not that we mean to do that, it just happens, because there's nowhere else for them to go at the time. Emma stuffed her inner child away and adopted the role of the fixer in the family.

When we're fixing things for our parents, we naturally become enmeshed and co-dependent with them. We're responsible for their happiness and not our own. Becoming a little parent made Emma feel in control and worthwhile. Her self-esteem was based on being sensible, good, practical and mature beyond her years.

But Emma was wearing a mask and when she lost her inner child, she lost her authentic self too. The need to be perfect was ever-present for her and it became hard to connect meaningfully with her friends. She could be in a room full of people but feel as though she was watching life pass her by from behind a screen. She was afraid of intimacy and of being seen for who she truly was. If she wasn't perfect, was she still lovable?

Emma had lost sight of what it means to be fundamentally human, and we're doing that all the time...

We're all perfectly imperfect. We get it wrong, we're messy and we need to be able to ask for help when we need it. Emma was terrified of being vulnerable and frightened to look within...

'There is a sweet surrender that comes from suspending
the internal chatter of old programming
to just allow the beauty of our flawed human-ness to breathe.
And to invite the 360-degree experience of love into our lives
and let it be enough.
Just as we are...
all very simply and beautifully enough.
Stumbling and Rising...
Perfectly Imperfect.'

Meeting Your Inner Child

Taking the time to meet your hidden child, not only intellectually from your mind but with the full power of your heart energy, is another radical act of self-love.

'It is safe to look within.
We often are frightened to look within because we think that we
will find this terrible being, but in spite of what they might have told
us, what we will find is a beautiful child that longs for our love.

*'As I move through the layers of other people's opinions and beliefs,
I see within myself a magnificent being, wise and beautiful.
I love what I see in myself.'*
LOUISE HAY

The hidden child longs to be known. As soon as I answer the front door to someone whose inner child is out in the cold, abandoned in the Shadowlands, they're there, tugging at my sleeve and chattering in my ear. I can hear their little clamouring voice and get snapshot images of them.

'I'm in the dark,' they say, mournfully. 'Let them know I'm here, they've forgotten me.'

'I'll do the best I can,' I reply, quietly settling into the session. I've got precisely 60 minutes to get them into the room and back into my client's heart space. They wait outside in the corridor to see if I manage it.

'I'm here for the little you,' I tell my client. 'Right now, I'm in service to them. If we don't invite them back in, they'll be left out in the cold... '

What happens then? When our orphaned inner child is in charge in the shadows, they can lash out, sabotage our relationships and wreak havoc in our lives from behind the scenes. This child is like a dangerous and unruly puppet-master entrusted with far too much power and responsibility. The truth is they want *us* to be responsible, to be adult and to take control of the emotional merry-go-round they got left having to navigate when they were separated from us in the first place.

You've already been growing your 'compassionate adult', who will hold your inner child safe. You're learning how to maintain kindness daily and how to listen with compassion. You're learning how to listen to what is spoken and what is unspoken. It's time to listen to your inner child.

Inner Child Reconnection

So now I'd like to invite you to take both hands and place them on your emotional heart in the centre of your chest.

You can imagine I am with you and we're doing this together.

Let's take five deep breaths. Close your mouth and inhale deeply through your nose and then open your mouth to release the breath with a deep sigh. Remember this isn't a superficial exhalation, it's a deep sigh.

Feel your feet on the ground or your back touching something solid behind you if you are sitting cross-legged.

You are here to meet your eight-year-old self.

Whether you've done inner child work before or not at all, *right here, right now*, you're reading these words to resource both your adult and your younger self with *more love...*

Take your heart-mind awareness to your childhood home. Imagine that you're standing outside the front door. Notice the colour and any defining features, like a bell, knocker, letterbox or number. Then repeat this statement:

'Dear inner child of mine,

I am here at the threshold to recover you completely.

I come with an open heart to listen with compassion to your story.

In the past, people hurt us.

I am here to validate your feelings and hold you with all of my love, warmth and kindness. I am here for our healing.

Know that I will keep you safe now and
will never leave your side again.

In love and light,

In love and light,

In love and light,

Blessed Be/Amen/Ase.'

Push the door open and step over the threshold.

You will find your inner child in this house. Which room are they in? As you approach your eight-year-old self, notice what they're wearing and the style of their hair. Trace the contours of their eyes, cheeks and hairline with your heart-mind.

What are they doing in this room? Are they playing, staring out of a window or watching TV? Do they have their back to you or are they facing you? What can you intuit about how they're feeling?

Make contact with your eight-year-old self. Sit beside them and put an arm around their shoulders or hold them to your heart in a warm embrace. Ask them how they are and what's happening for them at home and at school. Let them tell you their story.

Conclude by carrying them out of the room into the bright sunshine. Visualize both of you lying down in a beautiful meadow of soft green grass. Let your inner child know that you've got this. Tell them that they are safe now. You've come back to take them home and bring them back into your heart.

Gently open your eyes.

Journal Prompts

Write about your experience. Here are some points to reflect upon:

∗   How did you feel entering your childhood home? How did it feel seeing your eight-year-old self? What did they tell you about their life? What were they feeling about their parents, siblings, friends, teachers, the universe?

∗   Also write about what you remember about that time from your adult perspective. Name all of the people who were negatively or positively impacting your physical and mental wellbeing at this age. Reflect on how people spoke to you and the messaging behind their words. Were you being ridiculed, shamed or bullied by anyone?

∗   Give permission for all your feelings to bubble up to the surface. When you need to, tell yourself that it wasn't your fault. That you were a child, and whoever hurt you was wounded themselves and now you release them fully from every part of your being with love.

∗   Make a note of the situations, people, trauma and emotions you are choosing to release and burn it on a Full Moon.

The arrival of my inner child was subtle yet powerful. It began with a soft voice in my heart, inviting me to reconnect with the innocence and vulnerability that I had long suppressed. As I went deeper into the process, my inner child gradually revealed herself to me in various ways. I could sense her emotions through waves of memories, joy and deep, deep sadness.

Janice

I recall the session when we started to acknowledge my inner child. Observing her experience of life, I felt tremendous love and compassion for her. I remember the darkness and the dark grey energy that surrounded me in those days, the depression that I carried around for many years.

In my career, I understood concepts quickly and was able to apply them. Where I struggled was with speaking up in meetings, even though I had lots to say. I also struggled with being able to negotiate or demand or ask others to complete work for me, whilst on a personal level, I just never had the guts to stand up to my bullying sister and let her get her way 99 per cent of the time.

I realized so many things in that session, and the greatest revelation was that my fear of speaking up was tied to my mother, and the wrath she experienced when she raised her voice against my dad.

Erika

The hidden child longs to be seen, heard and acknowledged. They yearn for a feeling of safety... They just want to curl up in the palm of our hand, on our lap or in our heart and be loved and protected by us for the rest of our days here. And to have fun!

Fun with the Inner Child

Over the next few days or weeks, spend more time with your eight-year-old inner child. Regularly ask them how they are feeling and what they need.

Keep an inner child diary. Indulge them with anything from eating their favourite food to reconnecting with the TV shows that they watched at that time.

Take your inner child out with you to do things that are fun and nourishing. Make sure you ask them how they would like to spend the day – give them permission to be as playful as they want to be. You are creating a safe space for a return to the full expression of your joy, creativity and wonder.

Whenever you find that your inner child is disturbed, angry or sad, ask why they are feeling these emotions and be sure to listen to what they say. Journal their responses and in your heart-mind weave a cocoon of golden light around them, invite them back into your heart and place them in this safe space.

Over the next few weeks or months, repeat this practice to meet yourself at different ages. Go back and connect with your baby self and your three-, six- and twelve-year-old selves. Then find your teenager. Allow your heart to intuitively guide you to the age that's most important for you. It may not work out chronologically. Trust the process.

You may find your inner child is cold and unresponsive to you. This will be temporary. Return to them with patience, compassion and lots and lots of love.

Take as much time as you need to meet, recover and integrate these younger selves. There's absolutely no rush to complete this work. You can continue the True Essence Process whilst still working through different aspects of it.

As I sat in my London flat, consumed by the bleakness of the lonely English winter, I decided to be proactive and do what I've always done when I'm feeling low: seek a spiritual outlet. And so, like any good Gen Z-er, I reached for my phone and searched 'Best energy healers near me'.

A quick search led me to the acclaimed 'heart whisperer' Estelle Bingham. Fresh off the train from Paddington station, I walked to her address, where she took me upstairs to her workspace and began guiding me through a visual meditation.

After working our way through six of my seven chakras, we turned our attention to my heart chakra, the showpiece of Estelle's gift.

The meditative work on my heart centre felt metamorphic, and once Estelle had guided me back to the present, she looked at me sternly as I tried to ease the palpable tension with humour and witticisms. She asked me what emotions had arisen during the meditation.

After ample processing time, I responded, 'Loss.'

She nodded her head slightly and asked, 'What happened when you were three?'

Instantly my heart dropped, as the memories, night terrors and familiar and overwhelming sense of shame that I worked so hard to repress flooded my body and mind. There I was again, a three-year-old girl suffering abuse, attempting to make sense of something insidious, unfathomable and utterly isolating.

Estelle allowed me to hold space for that three-year-old girl and give her what she had needed back when the abuse happened.

This prescription – protection, empathy, and the knowledge that the shame I had silently suffered was not mine to claim – helped me free myself from it.

My personal experience of abuse eventually led me to the academic pursuits, professional experience and survivor-centred advocacy that have prepared me for law school and a career focused on gender and reproductive justice.

At the end of my healing session, Estelle embraced me and told me I would alchemize the experiences of my childhood.

Since that hour spent in the home of the British heart whisperer, I've stood in my truth and cultivated compassion for myself.

Tiger Lily

Compassion, Compassion, Compassion!

Surrender to the divine quality of compassion. Embrace it. Actually, choose to bring it on in truckloads! Because you're human and perfectly imperfect. And some days will be better than others.

So, treat yourself with sweetness. Allow yourself to put one foot in front of the other, and if you fall, help yourself up again.

Compassion for yourself is integral to the alchemy of the heart. Compassion is the mother of all mothers and the father of all fathers. It's the most *loyal, enduring* and *constant* of companions.

When we fall, compassion is there by our side to lovingly help us up. To dust us down when we feel unworthy of care.

When we are haunted by our perceived flaws and imperfections, compassion is the shoulder, the lap, the wide embrace.

Compassion doesn't sit in judgement. Compassion exudes sweetness, grace and purity.

Compassion allows us to be kind to ourselves. It mops brows. Holds hands. It cradles us and rocks us and dries our tears.

Come as you are to the feet of compassion. There are no sign-up fees or hidden charges here!

Above all, have compassion for yourself. After all, you've shown up. You're here for the challenge. For the change. For the possibility of a new reality.

Inner Child Healing

'Healing is... letting your inner child tell their story.'

Locating, listening to and reparenting this younger part of yourself will pave the way for extraordinary healing and transformation.

Whilst you are doing this work, find a picture of yourself as a child and create an altar around the image. Light a candle daily to create sacred space when you are working with the spirit of your hidden child. This is a candle that is honouring their story.

Ashley decided to heal and came on one of my men's retreats:

It started at the age of two, when my dad left, and then I lost Mum at the age of five, and it felt incredibly liberating but also extraordinarily tough to acknowledge what I went through. The most powerful outcome of it was understanding and giving a licence to the way I feel now as an adult. Why do I constantly feel I'm reaching, I'm looking for attention and looking to be seen and heard, and when I'm not, I get super-frustrated?

Healing is letting your inner child tell their story. Locating, listening to and reparenting this younger part of yourself will pave the way for extraordinary healing and transformation.

I felt that I was invisible, and carrying this sense of being a burden, and no one really knew what to do with me... My grandparents told me my stepmum was a witch and I wasn't allowed to have a picture of my mum, even though I wanted to treasure her memory. This wasn't a normal way to grow up, and now I know it's okay to feel it wasn't okay and feel all of those emotions that I've never acknowledged. I'm leaning more and more into them and now I have a toolbox, a framework to use to reflect on why I'm behaving the way I'm behaving, particularly in my relationship with my partner and with my stepmum...

Yeah, get out of your head and get into your heart. I'd spent 49 years in my head, completely stuck in my head. It's very raw, very pure, very honest with your heart, and ultimately being in my heart finally facilitated my trauma-healing experience.

Ashley

Ashley hadn't had access to the tools, time or safe space to process the profound shock, confusion and grief he'd felt from losing his mum. His unexpressed emotions had been pushed into the Shadowlands, along with his five-year-old self, who was stuck in a frozen trauma state. Ashley had become an emotional survivalist, shut down his heart and retreated into the desert.

When we went into his emotional heart to recover his five-year-old self, adult Ashley gave permission for little Ashley to feel again. He told him, 'Of course you're sad, afraid and in shock. You miss Mummy and it's okay to miss Mummy. We love Mummy. You're safe now – I'm here. I've come back for you, I've got you and I'll never leave you again.'

If we've exited our emotional heart at an early age, we have such limited language for our feeling states. We can't describe or express our emotions. They feel overwhelming and alien to us. But by journeying into his emotional heart, Ashley was able to voice both the emotions of his five-year-old self and the validating words of his compassionate adult. This was the medicine his soul needed.

This is something I see so often. During Janice's healing, we dropped into her emotional heart and found little Janice in the darkness, very lonely and very sad...

Before going on the retreat, I didn't fully realize the importance of my inner child in my life. While I had heard about its importance for healing before, I hadn't taken the time to explore its significance. However, during that life-changing weekend, something profound happened, and my inner child started to emerge from the dark place where she had been stuck for many years...

The healing journey transformed and healed my inner child in ways I never thought were needed, let alone possible. It felt like the wounds of my past were finally acknowledged and I was embraced and gently comforted... My inner child found a safe place to express herself honestly and step out from the darkness, surrounded by so much light and love.

In the days and weeks that followed, I experienced a deep inner peace, with the laughter of my inner child resonating in the depths of my heart. This healing became a catalyst, setting in motion a series of transformative changes in my life...

As for my inner child's current whereabouts, she lives within me as an eternal part of who I am. She reminds me constantly of the importance of nurturing

and cherishing the childlike wonder that exists in each of us. She has become
my guiding compass, leading me towards a life that is genuine and fulfilling...

Janice

What had happened to Janice? Her mother had been very young when she had her and found her daughter's needs overwhelming. She would regularly resort to locking Janice in her room in the dark. Janice would cry herself to sleep on the floor by her bedroom door. When we found little Janice, she was stuck in that place. Traumatized and confused by her mother's neglect, she felt unlovable to the core of her being.

In that session we were retrieving this aspect of Janice from the darkness. When I spoke to her recently, she remembered a very strong tingling sensation along the left-hand side of her body and a profound sense of being connected to oceans of bliss. She also spoke about how, since recovering her hidden child, she had met a partner who was unlike anyone she had met before. Previously her partners had been narcissists or displayed narcissistic traits. These men obviously mirrored her belief that she was unworthy of love. Today she is looking into a very different mirror. In this mirror she is beautiful inside and out. She is worthy.

Little Janice was scooped up and brought into the light. She was gifted with a soft, safe place in a pocket of Janice's heart forever.

Not only does this recovery of the inner child change what we can manifest in our lives, but it also replaces feelings of despair, defeat, low-level depression, emptiness and disenchantment with a blissful aliveness.

I embraced my inner child. She needed to be assured that there was love in
this world. I hugged her and felt overwhelming love for her.

I remember speaking to her and consoling her. I told her everything was going to be okay and that she didn't need to be afraid any longer. The fear was a protection mechanism that I no longer needed.

Walking out of the room that day, I felt complete and at peace. I also found my voice...

Erika

You have the right to make something beautiful from the broken pieces of your childhood stories. To turn the shards into something wonderful. No one can ever take that power away from you. So, begin today. Tap into that power.

> *'You suppose you are the trouble. But you are the cure.*
> *You suppose that you are the lock on the door.*
> *But you are the key that opens it.*
> *It's too bad that you want to be someone else.*
> *You don't see your own face, your own beauty.*
> *Yet no face is more beautiful than yours.'*
>
> RUMI

Slowly I started to speak up. The results were cumulative, consistent and quick. Fast-forward a few years and I now manage a global team of 20 and have no qualms about directing my team and ensuring we collectively manage our deliverables.

On a personal level, my sister and I have a very different relationship now – I push back with solid boundaries and give as good as I get and I love it!

Estelle has given me the ability to feel so empowered in the areas of my life where I felt blocked, and I am so grateful.

Another significant impact has been the change in the way that I speak to myself. I recall having negative thoughts about myself, which I have stopped because I am talking to myself in a kinder way now.

The whole experience with this heart-embodied healing has fostered more self-love than I would have ever thought was possible.

Erika

Love and Compassion

There is something to be said for walking full circle back into the arms of love. It didn't go anywhere. It has been here all along. In Sufism, the dervish reminds us of the circle, the dance back to the Source, the spiral into the infinite of the Creator – whirling into *love*. Into union, into bliss.

It's interesting how the word 'bliss' can make people feel uncomfortable. The idea of perfect happiness, a state of spiritual blessedness, can feel somehow way too idealistic, the stuff of far-flung fantasy. Or maybe it's just a bit too New Agey and sixties sounding?

Find a pen and jot down what bliss really means to you. Have you ever experienced bliss? Do you think you will experience bliss again?

The bliss state is actually a peace state. It's about suspending fear momentarily and showing up to each moment in truthfulness.

Remember that a negative childhood experience often creates an ego that will ultimately wreak havoc on our joy unless we step into the fray, wrestle it to the ground and put it back out to pasture.

There is something to be
said for walking full circle
back into the arms of love.
It didn't go anywhere.
It's been here all along.

Journal Prompts

* Plot your life like a path from the very beginning to this moment. Write your date of birth and then the most significant events that happened to you during your childhood and your teens.

* Think about all of the relationships where there was love, or a lack of it. They are like forks in the road. What did you choose? To honour your preciousness or to compromise it? How will you support yourself today to set the child free? Dance, sing, paint, discover...

I was in my mid-thirties, around seven years sober, when another relationship with an unavailable man ended and his betrayal triggered such huge feelings that locked-away memories of childhood sexual abuse began resurfacing. This was pain I had no idea it was possible to bear.

I was diagnosed with complex PTSD and clinical depression. I went to a centre in Arizona to do some trauma work, and when I arrived, I completely fell apart. I ended up on suicide watch and copious amounts of medication.

One of the questions the therapists asked me was why I wasn't willing to turn my life over to something else, why I felt I had to always be in control... What I discovered was that I had no trust in anything else because of what had happened to me as a child. This, however painful, was the beginning of what I call my spiritual journey.

Fast-forward a few years. I was a newly divorced single mother, Estelle came into my life and my healing journey began. It has taken 12 years, but I've been able to uncover parts of myself and heal in a way that I never thought possible.

In the first few years of working with Estelle, I was able to build a connection with something else, but was still unsure what. Through healing journeys, I met my spirit guides and was taken to different dimensions. All of this helped me build the belief that I wasn't on my own.

I fell in love during this time, and for a while all was wonderful, but my unresolved trauma and love addiction took over and... I ended up in a very dark place and back on meds. Finally I realized that I was the one common thread in all of these toxic relationships, and that I needed to become accountable. I went on Estelle's Love Retreat and really connected to my heart properly for the first time. The loving intimacy and safety of the space on the retreat and the work I had done before with her helped me to let go of the abuser and his energy, and I have never been triggered in the same way since that day.

Last year, another horrific abuse memory came up, something I had a sense was there, but it was now time for me to process it. A huge amount of grief came up, and I thought I was sinking again. A few months after, I had another healing with Estelle and her practitioners... In that session... the little girl in me who was never seen, held or heard, finally was.

From that day, my voice changed – it became much deeper, like finally my adult was leading me. Having always been a victim, and that being my unconscious pattern so that I didn't have to be responsible and thrive, I am now in my power and have a voice. I have such a strength in me. Obviously things happen, because I'm human, but my thought processes are so different and come from a place of faith and knowing. I'm able to turn up for myself and others and love life and all that it offers...

Jenny

The truth is that turning up for ourselves and having compassion for ourselves are non-negotiable. Without presence and compassion, we are doomed to powering a self-effacing, self-defeating karmic wheel of punishment and sabotage. Yet our time on the Earth plane presents us with the opportunity to integrate and grow beyond the limitations of the ego to connect with our higher self, our True Essence. This is known as self-realization.

But for now, back to love. Love yourself. Love everything you do. And be kind. Be kind to yourself. Especially in the difficult moments. We all have them. We all have emotional triggers. What triggers us depends on our unique history, childhood experiences and personality. But if we're ignoring our inner child, we find it impossible to self-regulate and respond functionally to our triggers.

Journal Prompts

* Engage your eagle-eyed observer and keep a diary of what triggers you.

* Notice if it feels as if you responded from the child version of yourself or your adult self.

* Spend some time reflecting on why your inner child was affected by the situation. Can you link it back to something similar that happened in your earlier life? Build a dialogue with your younger self and remind your inner child that you are in charge now and nothing from the past can come back to destroy your peace.

Understanding the root of your triggers will help you integrate and heal them. Whenever you find yourself triggered, try using your five senses to physically ground yourself:

Grounding through the Senses

Take a moment to identify:

~ five things that you can see

~ four things that you can touch

~ three things that you can hear

~ two things that you can smell

~ one thing that you can taste

This grounding exercise allows your brain to focus on something other than what has triggered you. When you combine this with deep breathing, you will return to a sense of calm in your body.

You can also restore a sense of calm by letting go of what no longer serves you.

The Slipstream of Compassion

Close your eyes and imagine you are sitting on the bank of a river that flows from a glacier high up in a mystical mountain range.

Notice the sounds of the birds and the murmur of the wind through the leaves on the trees behind you and on the opposite bank.

Visualize this etheric energy washing through you and inhale its strength into your physical, emotional and spiritual bodies.

This body of water is powerful and pure. Listen to the sound of its life-force as it flows past you.

Take your heart-mind to the chakras or places in your body where you feel you are still holding stagnant or stuck energy from your childhood. As you breathe, imagine that energy washing out of your body into the river and back to the ocean.

Imagine the members of your family one by one and think about where you are holding them in your energy body. Let them go one by one.

Journal Prompts

* Notice how your heart feels and what emotions emerge.

* Notice if you feel a need to cry, and if so, what emotion is looking to express itself through your tears. Is it grief, sadness, relief or fear?

* Do you have an urge to suppress your emerging feelings?

* Can you give permission for all your feelings to flow?

* What does it feel like when you lean into the release here?

* Did you see your inner child? If so, describe where they were and what they were doing.

I taught myself at a young age that being emotional was akin to being 'needy' and that this was a sign of weakness. To use a wholly accurate way to sum up how I felt, I was repulsed by the idea of being needy of anyone or anything.

Physically repulsed. I did not, interestingly, feel that others were needy to the same degree. This harsh verdict was reserved solely for myself...

The first time I realized I needed help was when I became a mother. I was taken aback by the shift in my hormones. The 'baby blues' hit me hard and caused all sorts of uncontrollable emotional upheaval... I was petrified I would be a bad mother.

By the time my second daughter was born, I was fairly messed up. I was projecting my fears onto both my daughters, being overly protective, overcompensating, allowing them to show their feelings while pushing my own out of the way, which of course made me more closed to them.

I found numerous professionals over the years (therapists, psychologists, psychoanalysts)... but the really great thing about all these traditional therapies was that I could avoid talking about anything real...

And so, when perimenopause was upon me and I felt generally deflated and devoid of energy and knew I still needed to sort myself out, I decided to google some more holistic forms of healing...

I almost didn't go to my first appointment with Estelle, but she saw me and she was right about everything she said then and she has been right about everything she has said subsequently.

As I was leaving, she casually mentioned that she had a place available on a retreat she was hosting that very weekend, and that I should come...

On the last day of the retreat I experienced an awakening of sorts, experiencing first-hand the meaning of trust and safety. And of letting go. Letting go of the painful need to hold everything in check and push it down, letting go of the tears that needed to flow, letting go of my fear of being needy, my dislike of being touched, my disdain for my own needs, of all the survival skills that no longer served me... I felt loved, and I felt love for everyone else.

Michelle

Integration

The process of integration doesn't happen overnight, but will unfurl over time. Integration is at the core of inner child healing because when we give ourselves permission to acknowledge our wounds and spend time with the feelings that emerge from them, we are learning how to parent ourselves.

> *'Wholeness is not achieved by cutting off a portion of one's being, but by integration of the contraries.'*
> CARL JUNG

Integrating Core Wounds

Take your journal and everything you need in the moment.

Read this list of core wounds and identify which ones resonate with you: abandonment, betrayal, rejection/neglect, humiliation, injustice, physical/sexual abuse, psychological/emotional/verbal abuse.

Where there is one wound, there will often be another one lurking just behind it. So, if we've been rejected as children, we'll also carry the abandonment wound, and if we've been abused in some way, we'll also suffer from abandonment, rejection and betrayal. So, you are probably holding a combination of wounds in your emotional body.

Today you're choosing one core wound to work with.

~ Write the word down in the middle of a page of your journal and draw a circle around it.

~ Close your eyes, breathe into your heart, drop into the energy of that wound and ask yourself how it feels and how it makes you feel in your life. Draw lines out of your wound circle and add the feelings that you have acknowledged.

~ Write a list of all the things that you don't like about yourself and relate them back to your core wounding. Know that you can let go of these judgements.

~ Listen to your inner child with love and non-judgement and be mindful of and attentive to all of the feelings and memories that emerge.

~ Write a love letter to your inner child and make sure you tell them everything that they didn't hear in your childhood. This is your opportunity to heal in a deep way. Read it back to yourself at night whilst you are working with your inner child.

~ Take your inner child with you when you go out into the world. Integrated. At one. At peace.

CHAPTER 6

Meeting Shame at the Door

'This being human is a guest house.
Every morning a new arrival.

A joy, a depression, a meanness,
some momentary awareness comes
as an unexpected visitor.

Welcome and entertain them all!
Even if they're a crowd of sorrows,
who violently sweep your house
empty of its furniture,
still, treat each guest honourably.
He may be clearing you out
for some new delight.

The dark thought, the shame, the malice,
meet them at the door laughing, and invite them in.'
RUMI, 'THE GUEST HOUSE'

The universe conspires to bring you home. Any way it can. It will break you down to crack you open. It will trip you up to pick you up. It will send you lessons, tests and a few dark nights of the soul. You'll receive all manner of messages that only you can decipher and synchronicities that you can't rationalize away.

How many times have you seen 11:11 this month? Numbers, cloud formations, white feathers, random meetings, pocket calls, insects, birds, the perfect song at the perfect moment, you name it, your higher self is in this for the long haul and wants you to wake up to the truth of who you are!

You're a remarkable being with so much to give and so much to do, and the time we spend in this dimension is over in the flash of an eye. Remember it's an adventure. You chose to come back, you chose to evolve, you chose to call in the people, places and experiences that would help you do just that... and now you can choose to change your life.

You're already doing an amazing job. You've stepped into your emotional heart. You've integrated banished parts of yourself, triggers and projections. You've recovered your hidden child. You've alchemized blocks from the past.

You're not your past. You're not your thoughts – they're constructs of the mind. Your emotions come and go. This *now*, this *right here, right now* is the only reality. *This* is where the magic happens.

•••

This pilgrimage into the heart has also brought you into a new type of relationship with shame. You may have encountered it in the Shadowlands or at different moments with your inner child.

And so I was about to leave it there, but then I felt a wilful and defiant tugging at the corner of my awareness. Shame announced itself and said to me in no uncertain terms, 'I deserve a moment of my own.'

And I stood to attention. I listened intently. I looked shame in the eye, and after a pause, I said, 'Yes, I do believe that you do.'

Meeting Shame

'Shame has arrived at the door.
Here is the unholy visitor who will crash the party before it's even started.
Proud owner of your life records,
shame will crush you with memories of
perceived mistakes and indiscretions,
choking you with a litany of flaws and a catalogue of critical observations.
Shame will speak to you in a language that only you can understand...
of how you're "too damaged", "too much" or "not enough".
"Who are you to dare think you can change,
heal, love or be loved?" it will say...'

'I don't feel shame.'

I'm sitting in a session with a client who doesn't remember her childhood and readily admits that she doesn't feel.

Masking or pretending can become our default mode because shame cuts us off from our own emotions. We don't feel it, but that's because we don't feel anything.

Others find it difficult to connect with their sense of shame because it lies hidden beneath so many other emotions. But look under that very heavy slab of rock in the darkest part of the Shadowlands, and I can guarantee that you'll find our friend shame hanging out there.

Shame is like a knotty thread, woven through everything we find in our Shadow. It's everywhere and in everything. Coiled tightly in our lost inner child, behind the voice of the relentless inner critic/judge/saboteur and beneath the rage. Our addictions, lack of purpose, self-loathing, sense of worthlessness and inability to use our voice to state our needs, truth or boundaries are symptoms of shame.

Are you that person who finds themselves pushing away the tears because crying in front of someone, being *vulnerable*, is your absolute worst nightmare? Well, yes, you guessed it, shame is in the mix.

Shame is a complex emotion, born of the internalized response to childhood or teenage trauma or disconnection, although we can accumulate it at any age. It's also impacted by deeply ingrained belief systems and societal or cultural expectations that shaped our sense of self in our formative years. So, think back to the rules and values of your religion, school, friendship group or larger social network. What were their values, norms and standards, and did you abide by them?

It's important to note here that there's a distinct difference between healthy shame and toxic shame. In *Healing the Shame That Binds You*, John Bradshaw refers to healthy shame as a 'basic metaphysical boundary for human beings'. Healthy shame is an emotional energy that 'gives us permission to be human, and signals to us that we are not God – that we *have* made and *will* make mistakes... that we need help.'

There's an ancient Greek myth that really sheds some light on this idea. It's about the master craftsman Daedalus and his son, Icarus, who have been imprisoned in a tower on the island of Crete. Daedalus designs two sets of wings from feathers and wax, so they can both escape over the sea. He warns Icarus not to fly too close to the sun or too low to the sea. Icarus doesn't listen to his father's warning and flies higher and higher towards the sun until his wings predictably melt and he tumbles into the ocean and dies.

This is a tragic story about healthy shame, and Icarus doesn't have any. He believes that he is perfect, infallible and that the laws of nature don't apply to him. This oversight seals his fate.

Healthy shame is a powerful glue that holds society together because it teaches us about our limitations, how to make amends when we need to and, perhaps most importantly, how to learn from our mistakes. It helps us grow. We need to create space to recognize when we haven't made the best decisions, so that we can figure out how to improve them in the future. Healthy shame offers us that space – a moment to pause, reassess and reflect on our choices in a robust way.

Toxic shame is a different ball game.

•••

Our Little Pocket of Shame

We all have a little pocket of this energy tucked away somewhere deep inside. As Gershen Kaufman, a clinical psychologist who started writing about shame in the 1960s explains, it's an unavoidable part of being human, because it's so closely tied to our sense of abandonment, and everyone has some form of this wound:

*'Shame is inevitable when individuals interact,
precisely because we are human and therefore
behave in ways that have unintended impact.'*

We are all perfectly imperfect, so make mistakes and get things wrong every day. The damage happens in our childhood if the adults in our life ignore the hurtful things that they've done or said and we are left with feelings of abandonment, sadness or confusion.

The way around this is to build an interpersonal bridge at the time of the event. This bridge extends from the adult to the child to repair hurt or pain in the moment.

If this doesn't happen, the child *internalizes* their emotion, and this turns into a layer of toxic shame inside us. The internalized negative feelings are driven into the fabric of our identity. So, 'I did a bad thing' becomes 'I am a bad person.' Our subsequent negative self-talk can present as 'I'm stupid, I shouldn't have been born, I never get it right, I'm a failure, I hate myself, I'm worthless, defective, inadequate, inferior, small, not good enough...' and the list will go on. Toxic shame slides surreptitiously into the chamber of the emotional heart and settles in for the duration.

In his book *The Wild Edge of Sorrow*, which delves into the sacred work of grief, psychotherapist Francis Weller explores the origins of shame and says:

*'Every one of us has encountered times when the connection
between us and the one we needed for attention and love
was ruptured... with enough repetition, the internal stories
associated with those events reach their saturation point, and
the fictions crystalize into things that feel like truths.'*

Imagine arriving home as a child bursting with pride about a picture that you painted at school that day. You take it to a parent, but they're distracted or dismissive, busy sending a work email or making dinner. Your sense of self comes crashing down and you feel dejected, sad and embarrassed.

If the parent finds you at some point that day and explains their actions, apologizes and looks at the picture, saying something like, 'I'm so sorry I didn't look at your picture earlier. I had an email to send, but didn't explain that properly to you. It wasn't about you or the picture. I'm excited to look at it now. Well done,' then you won't absorb or hang on to the experience. You won't internalize the feelings because you'll process them at the time and they'll just flow through you.

If the experience is never addressed, however, you go to sleep believing that you're wrong on all levels. You'll swallow your feelings of confusion, anger, fear, sadness and abandonment and they'll become a layer of toxic shame within you.

> *'Shame corrodes the very part of us that*
> *believes we are capable of change.'*
> **Brené Brown**

This also happens if we have immature parents or siblings who hijack the emotional space in the house with their constant drama. We get used to taking up very little or no space at all and habitually internalizing everything we feel.

Another example is if our family or school environment is emotionally phobic. As children, we're experiencing different emotions about things all the time as we interact more and more with a world that is still new to us. But if there are no adults around us modelling how to feel or process emotion in a safe, grounded and loving way, then we end up believing that our feelings are wrong.

We need to know that all our feelings are valid and learn through our relationships with adults how to robustly honour, express and mentalize them.

Anything from experiencing grief about a rabbit or a grandparent passing away to having an argument with a friend at school to watching something scary on TV can make us feel insecure and lonely. If there's nowhere to go with our feelings, we stuff them away and continue an ancestral cycle. They are our core wounds. We become emotionally phobic as adults and can find it difficult to feel or find the words to express what we're feeling, but get triggered instead. We naturally invalidate the truth of our experiences and will find ourselves in relationships that mirror this pattern.

If we want to heal, we must invite shame to cross the threshold.

The Invitation

Offer shame a hand, a warm embrace. Bring it inside. Sit down with it like old friends and be kind.

In doing so, you will unravel the old stories and 'fictions' that felt 'like truths' and forgive yourself over and over again for the things that were never your fault.

It will be Love, the greatest of all medicines, that will finally soothe this hollow-eyed spectre, and compassion, the most alchemical of all balms, that will sweeten the toxic chatter and dissolve the invisible power of the unholy visitor and the layers of toxic shame that sit in the darkest corners of your emotional heart.

And you will understand, when all is said and done, that shame wasn't so unholy after all. Shame always had a place at the table, and when invited to sit there, it has the potential to transform, like all our other exiled and deeply maligned parts. Shame is perhaps the greatest of all our guides from beyond.

•••

I'm sitting cross-legged in the opening circle of the Love Retreat. We're a group of strangers nestled in an 11th-century friary deep in the English countryside, overlooking a lake and surrounded by acres of ancient woodland. The autumn evening has drawn in around us and the warm glow of the fire is now casting long shadows on the walls and illuminating the intricate crisscross of the beautiful Gothic mullion windows. This is a time of complete immersion into the heart, and miracles happen here.

The Love Retreat

Spirit guided me to create this container for the Divine Feminine, and it's *her* slipstream of infinite Love and compassion that's channelled through it. This container is a portal for her energy to touch down into this dimension.

The Divine Feminine is within all of us and it's the embodying of that truth that moves people to the edges of themselves and beyond, into the beauty of their True Essence.

The heart has its ways, so kind, so strong, so bold and full of knowing, and I notice that there's always a moment over the course of the weekend when each person becomes startled and then profoundly humbled by the true face of Love – a face that's mirrored back to them by the other, by the whole and by themselves, despite their negative self-talk and belief systems.

When a group comes together for soul work it always chooses itself, and the Love Retreat is no exception to this rule. These souls believe that they're strangers, but they will share karma and mirror wounds and stories. There are sacred contracts here. These brave souls have all chosen to step into their emotional heart in this way, at this time, for a reason. And the reason is always specific to the group.

As I sink into the stillness and the mystery, the reason is beginning to make itself very clear to me. A theme has steadily begun to emerge. It's knocking at the door and demanding our attention. Shame is here, looking to meet us at the threshold...

I'm sitting in a circle and Estelle has just guided me into my heart space...

I'm immediately terrified, worried about how my body language looks to the others but simply not able to draw my knees from my chest. Heart racing, I feel childish, unsure and out of my depth. In my gut I know what's about to happen and it scares me. I'm going to have to 'be open'. Yet I chose this retreat, so I use this fact to talk myself off the ledge.

Everyone else in the room looks in various states of bewilderment too, which helps, and I can hear my brain saying, You can hide what you need to and just get through this weekend. *I remind myself this is not the right attitude... I dig my hands into the sheepskin seating and try to anchor myself.*

Estelle acknowledges the unease in the room, which eases the tension.

I have a rough start. My very first interaction is with a woman whose trauma echoes mine. In meeting her eyes, I feel a tsunami of anger, mistrust, judgement, hurt, shame, embarrassment and dislike. Since she looks as upset as I feel, I hold her gaze, but it's agonizing. I feel clumsy and wrong. I think, This is horrific. How do I leave? Where's the value in this?

The Divine Feminine is within all of us and it's the embodying of that truth that moves people to the edges of themselves and beyond, into the beauty of their True Essence.

But I continue, and it becomes clear that everyone has their own inner world and is trying their best to share it, some more successfully than others. Realizing this softens something in me.

I grapple with what I might need to get through the rest of this opening ceremony. A dear old friend suddenly comes to mind, one of the very few people in the world that I trust and that I believe really loves me, and I use her as a talisman.

Then I'm astounded by the immense love I'm suddenly feeling for the woman to my left, which is mind-exploding, since I've only just met her, have never held a conversation with her and only know her first name.

That night I write in my journal, 'Maybe I don't need to be so defensive?'

Kelly

Kelly's toxic shame told her that it wasn't safe to show up authentically and let us see her. We were confronting all the notions that she held in her Shadow about being intimate with others. We were facing her barricaded heart and challenging her to soften her defences and trust us with the stories that were buried in her emotional heart.

It was a huge leap of faith for her to stay present with the pain in the room, but with that first step she offered shame her hand, and this would pave the way for the healing and life-changing transformation that she experienced over the weekend.

What was happening elsewhere?

It's the morning after our opening circle and I've woken up ready to run. To say the first night was intense would be a huge understatement. My heart was opened by a group of strangers and I'm scared of what's going to happen next. And yet, despite the inherent need to escape, something deep within me is yelling that this is where I need to be.

Vic

If we're not living an authentic life, we constantly second-guess ourselves, worrying what other people are thinking about us. We're anxious, depressed and haunted by feelings of worthlessness. We're also petrified about dropping the mask that we present to the world, because this means we'll be found out. Vic believed that we wouldn't like or accept who she was without her mask. Just like Kelly, she assumed that if we encountered her authentic self, we would hurt, reject and abandon her. Both Kelly and Vic had grown up in families that invalidated or ignored their experiences and feelings.

Every cell in Vic's body was urging her to back out of her emotional heart and run for the hills. To return to the 'safety' of what she knew. To keep the heart barricaded. But her mystic heart, her soul, her higher self, her True Essence, was yelling at her to stay. She stayed.

When we take the time to step into the chamber of our emotional heart, it's extraordinary how deep we go. We're able to access the unified field of consciousness in a very short space of time. This unified field is quantum, so essentially this container, and the healing that happens in it, isn't constrained by space, time or the limitations of the mind. And isn't dependent on how much spiritual work people have done before either.

During the opening ceremony, I was filled with awe and discombobulation as I sat in the circle, feeling more exposed and transparent than ever before. There was nowhere to hide. As a group, we'd only known each other for an hour at most and I thought I was still firmly in the ego space of 'holding it all together'. But moments after Estelle guided us into our heart space, I was overwhelmed by the intense emotions buried deep within me instantaneously being thrust into the circle.

I remember trying to force a laugh, rolling my eyes, as if to say, 'Sorry for this ridiculous, over-the-top mess emerging from me. It's nothing, just ignore it.' But no one was going to ignore it or laugh with me. Each face held me with such sincere compassion. The shame, anger, fear and feeling of inadequacy suppressed within me since childhood was being seen, felt, compassionately held and, most importantly, not judged.

It was then that I realized we'd entered an intimate heart-opening portal that transcended ego and was taking us right to the essence of our souls' chosen healing journey – whether we liked it or not. There was no other way to be but surrendering to what was emerging through and around us.

Natalie

Natalie was aware of the chatter of her toxic shame, but still gave herself permission to surrender to the unfamiliar and scary reality of heart-embodied intimacy. Over the course of the weekend, she would trust herself and the process enough to bring her exiled hidden child in from the cold. She has been spending precious time with her ever since.

To heal, we can't *think* our feelings, we must *feel* our feelings. We must embody them to release them. The mind, the intellect, the talking about our feelings can only get us so far. To truly transform, we must *experience* our stories *with an open heart*. That's when everything changes.

You can also do this work alone, which is what you're doing right now. By spending time creating a safe sacred space, growing your compassionate adult and embodying compassion and courage, celebrating your authentic essential nature and manifesting your True Essence.

You are the container. Everything you need has always been within you.

Take a breath and say:

> 'I am sacred space. *Before this lifetime I came from sacred wholeness and today I honour this sacred truth.*'

As Vic voyaged deeper into her sacred heart space, she found her eight-year-old self waiting patiently for her to arrive. She had waited for many years, neglected in the Shadowlands, carrying feelings of sadness and resentment that had formed themselves into hatred and toxic shame.

> *I was unhappy as a child, and I can talk about the fact that I didn't enjoy school, that I was bullied and felt very lonely. But now, in our circle, what emerges is so much more. A photo of me at seven or eight years old keeps creeping into my mind. I am sitting crying and shivering on a beach. Capturing this child in a moment of deep sadness when all she needed was to be held hits me hard. My usual narrative is that I resent my family for not recognizing how I felt, but over the weekend I realize that I've been feeling hate. Hate has been my coping mechanism, an outlet for my emotions.*
>
> *Prominent in my thoughts and discussions are also feelings of guilt about how I parent my children. My fear is that I'm not good enough for them and ultimately that I will let them down. I continually fall back into the narrative that I'm not a good person and that's on display for everyone to see.*

Vic

It was time for Vic to connect with her own compassionate adult to lovingly acknowledge the lost little girl who was crying and shivering on a beach, with no idea how to make sense of how lonely, misunderstood and miserable she felt...

The space we held for one another on the last day was sacred, loving and safe. Surrounded by love, my intense feelings of shame emerged. My young child did not like herself; she did not want to be alive. My shame ran deep – feelings of not being good enough, of not being a good person, feelings that came from not feeling worthy. I felt a huge amount of shame for not protecting my young self and letting her be happy.

The space these beautiful women held for me allowed the shame to leave my body, piece by piece. We met resistance, because it had been held so deep for so long, but understanding and naming the intensity of my shame and releasing it by knowing none of this was my fault was a true blessing.

During our sessions, I experienced a tightness in my heart, which I now know was an opening up, allowing me to release the shame I had held on to for so long and allow my inner child to be happy.

I now feel I can embrace my children in a full and loving way. I feel a love and ease with myself that is wonderful.

Vic

Vic held a safe, nurturing internal space for her eight-year-old self to unravel the truth of her experience. She embodied pure love and compassion for herself when she acknowledged the deepest secret of all – that she hadn't wanted to be alive any more. She held this truth with a newfound tenderness and devotion to herself.

Over the course of these few days, she grasped the power of the heart space to unlock our innate ability to alchemize toxic shame into wisdom. She was able to forgive herself and become the healer and alchemist of her family line. She wouldn't be passing toxic shame down to her children. She was now free to love them without fear. We all have our stories...

The Face of Love

We are returning to the heart for a meditation and journalling session.

To create sacred space, light a candle, dedicating it to the divine spark that exists within you, the five elements that support life – Earth, Water, Fire, Air and Ether – and to God for this opportunity to empty more of what no longer serves you to make space for what does.

Place both hands on your heart area, close your eyes and take some long, slow heart-embodied breaths in through your nose and out through your mouth.

Imagine you are sitting underneath a waterfall of bright white or golden light.

Absorb this light frequency into every cell of your being. This light is cleansing your aura and washing away any unwanted energy or negativity.

On the next breath, call in the Divine Feminine with this invocation:

'In love and light,

In love and light,

In love and light,

I ask that the Divine Feminine be here now to support my healing and help me to dissolve all my toxic shame so that I might be free to be of service to the slipstream of compassion that exists within and without, a channel for love.

And so it is,

And so it is,

And so it is.

Blessed Be/Amen/Ase.'

Breathe and feel the golden light of divine Love surround you.

You may relate to the Divine Feminine in whichever way is the most comfortable for you. Perhaps you recognize her as Green Tara, Mother Mary, Sophia, Isis, Mary Magdalene, Oshun, Parvati or Kwan Yin. You can also connect with her as the Goddess, Mother Earth Pachamama or as one of the Celtic, Greek or Roman goddesses, like Brigid or Athena.

Ask her, the mother of all mothers, to help you meet shame at the threshold and reveal the specific pain point in your childhood that needs to be healed in this moment.

Wait to see what drops into your consciousness.

Spend a few moments with the images and then write about them in your journal.

This is a meditation that you can come back to for more guidance from the Divine Mother about other experiences that are creating cosmic shame and blocks in your life.

Journal Prompts

You can choose to journal one question at a time over a series of days or weeks if you need more time to process this work. Take what you need to resource yourself, self-regulate and self-soothe.

* Write about the experience that emerged for you during the meditation. Write about the emotions that you noticed that you were feeling at the time and what is happening in the body right now as you connect with this memory.

* Write about your childhood environment. Was it a safe place to explore and express your emotions?

* Were you shamed at home or at school about your sexuality, habits, preferences or your physical appearance? Reflect on a specific time in your life when that was happening to you. Take your time to connect with the experience and empty all the feelings out onto the page. Bring them into the light.

* Make a list of your shame-based thoughts and then reframe them. Ask your compassionate adult to help you. Use evidence to challenge your thoughts. So, the compassionate adult would say to Kelly and Vic, 'You have no evidence to prove that the other people in this room will harm you. The evidence that you have is that you are surrounded by love.' Sometimes we can't tell the difference, but by now you have been spending enough time in your heart space for your intuition to begin to guide you.

Dissolving the Power of Shame

'I was born when all I once feared I could love.'

RABIA, FEMALE SUFI MYSTIC, 717–801 CE

You might find that toxic shame is embedded in one particular area of your life. Some of my clients are super-successful at work but have massive blocks around sex and intimacy. For others, it's the other way around. Where do you thrive and where do you feel you are shut down?

Shame can manifest in many different ways, but the experience (or lack) of healthy intimacy in your life will give you a clear indication of where you're at with it.

Here are a few simple questions to ask yourself:

- How does the thought of true intimacy make me feel?

- How often am I vulnerable?

- Do I find it easy to ask for help? And how does it make me feel when I do?

- How much value do I place on what others think of me on a scale of 1 to 10 (1 being the least, 10 being the most)?

Some of you reading this will find toxic shame utterly consuming and it will be the lens through which you view the entire world. That lens is warped, but will inform all of your perceptions. It's like being in a crazy house of mirrors, a funfair attraction where everything is completely distorted. But rather than finding these reflections abnormal, you're totally signed up to them, swallowed alive by their energy.

> *'Imagine holding a fistful of broken glass tightly.*
> *This is toxic shame,*
> *silently tearing us into strips from the inside out.'*

How does this work out in practice?

My childhood was a very tough experience. My mum ran away from my dad when I was six months old, when she found out that she had MS. I lived in London, in a posh house in Hampstead, with my mum and grandma, but inside this house, my mother had lost her mobility and speech by the time I was seven and my grandma had severe dementia, ulcers and emphysema. She smoked 40 cigarettes a day and the house smelled badly of smoke. I was a carer for them both from a very young age.

It was so chaotic. I would come home from school and have to change my mum's incontinence pads and pressure sore dressings. I got everyone KFC for dinner every night with the money my dad gave me every week.

My dad was a very successful doctor who used to take me to visit his multiple girlfriends at the weekends and take me on luxury holidays, but for the most part I was a carer. Mum and Gran were rushed to hospital every year or two and were given a matter of months to survive, but they always survived.

I suppose shame came into being because at my expensive girls' school no one would have believed what I went home to every night.

When I was trying to do my A-levels, Mum was rushed to hospital and given months to live, so I had to split my time between hospital, school and home to check on my gran. I had got all 'A's for my GCSEs, but got all 'D's for my A-levels, and this set me on a path of not doing what I wanted in life. I put both my mum and gran into care homes when I was 18. I felt so guilty, but I couldn't care for them any more.

Anyway, I spent my twenties going to the nursing homes every weekend. My mum slowly deteriorated until for the last 10 years of her life she had locked-in syndrome. She was in her body, but couldn't really move or say anything. It was just horrendous, and Gran thought everyone was stealing from her and that I was her dad. At the same time, I was in a relationship with a narcissist.

The fact that their two souls were so connected set me off on my spiritual journey, but after they died, I felt a massive loss of purpose. I drank quite a lot at that time, and about two weeks afterwards I was out one night and someone put something in my drink and I was date-raped. I was just losing trust in the universe. Still, I soul-searched, went to music school and got a record deal. Then I lost the deal.

I slipped into a real depression. I got into a relationship with someone nine years younger than me, someone I didn't want to upset, and I felt completely stuck.

This was the state I was in when I arrived on Estelle's doorstep, pretending I was okay.

Anna

Anna had completely lost herself in the labyrinth of her childhood trauma. She loved her mother and grandmother very much, but their complex physical and mental health issues left her abjectly neglected. Her father chose to ignore that her home life was monumentally overwhelming, so no adult was validating her reality, helping to make it better or protecting her from it. This resulted in a deep well of toxic shame that was compounded by the traumatic events that followed.

After our first session, Anna went home, fell asleep in her boots and slept for 15 hours straight. She had been like a little bird, unable to land safely in the world. That day her emotional heart experienced such a great sense of relief that finally she could stop running and just be still. We all have our stories, and that day Anna was able to share hers...

After our first session, we continued the True Essence Process, healing, alchemizing and integrating aspects of her emotional heart. Today Anna is a yoga and movement teacher, married with a little girl and lives by the sea.

Give It Back!

The most dynamic and effective way to dissolve shame is to cease blaming yourself, to start forgiving yourself and to *give it back*!

Let's dissolve the burden of toxic shame:

- Forgive yourself for anything that was handed down to you by your parents, caregivers or school.

- Forgive yourself for your perceived failings and mistakes.

- Forgive yourself for any violations that happened to you.

- Forgive yourself for experiences that were out of your control.

- Forgive yourself for not knowing better or having the resources to make different choices at the time.

- Begin to affirm daily that you are forgiving yourself and letting go of this burden of toxic shame.

And as you release this burden and open up your emotional heart, you will become more in touch with your emotions and able to manifest more of your True Essence.

Embody Purpose, Power and Passion

Our emotions are vital to embodying our power, purpose and passion in this lifetime. They are the signposts to our most basic needs and galvanize us into action. Listening to what they're communicating and what's happening in our body is an act of self-love:

- Sadness puts us in contact with the truth of our emotional losses and our grief. It connects us to reality. It's essential for healing and developing compassion.

- Fear signals danger and teaches us about discernment.

- Guilt is the companion of our conscience. It keeps us connected to our values.

- Joy signals that we are well!

- Shame reminds us of our limitations.

- Anger helps us to recognize injustice and create boundaries by speaking our truth, and protecting and standing up for ourselves, our loved ones and what we believe in.

Now is the time to cherish the beauty
of your darkness and your light.
You're learning how to hold yourself
safe while you open yourself up to the
full expression of your soul's rainbow.

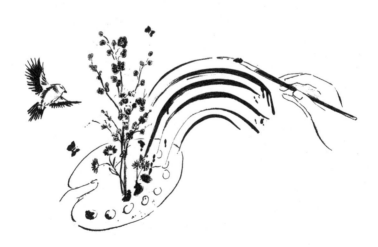

I often use the analogy of an artist's palette when describing emotion in sessions. Each of us has a palette of emotion within us, like a spectrum of colour. You can imagine it now. At one end of this spectrum is the inky black of the darkest night and this fans all the way through to the white of this page.

There is every conceivable shade in between, from the most beautiful purples, pinks, magentas and reds to sunrise oranges, yellows, emerald greens, browns and blues. And we need each colour to experience the fullness of the others. There is no light without dark, and emotion is the same. The colour black is made from mixing equal parts of red, blue and yellow together, and white light is a combination of all the colours of the rainbow.

When we're afraid to explore the full gamut of our emotions or have become alienated from them, we sit in the middle of our palette in a state of paralysis, frightened of integrating our darker emotions and blocked from truly experiencing the joy of our lighter ones.

You are the Divine incarnate and each area of your emotional heart that you embody is setting you free to become all that you were meant to be. Now is the time to cherish the beauty of your darkness and your light. You are learning how to hold yourself safe whilst you sit with uncomfortable feelings and open yourself up to the full expression of your soul's rainbow. Everyone you meet will feel the full colour, vibrancy and authenticity that you're embodying – and we can't wait to meet you!

CHAPTER 7

The Legacy of the Ancestors

'The voices of the ancestors echo within you.
In the stillness, the spaces in between the spaces...
you will find them.

Resting between each heartbeat,
they are embedded in the sinews of the body,
the rush of blood, etched into bone.

The ancestors call to us from the deepest
recesses of our being...
from beyond the hollow cave of self.'

My cousin Andrew had a recurring dream from a very early age. In this dream, Andrew is not in his body. He's with his younger brother, Stephen, and a cousin, who are also not in their bodies. They're in what feels like a waiting or holding area, preparing to be born again.

'We knew we were going into another realm, into another existence,' he told me, 'and we were quite excited about it. I remember the most amazing orange light, and it made me feel incredibly peaceful. This area looked like a type of runway leading to a sunset. This was the place we were headed to for our next lifetime. It didn't feel like a dream. I'm convinced it happened.'

To me, the thought of these three souls choosing to be together again is so moving and comforting, but I've found that some of my clients can really struggle with the idea that we choose our families and lives. I appreciate that this is especially difficult if you've experienced hardship, suffering or abuse within your family system. The idea that you've willingly signed up to a life with people who will cause you harm can feel exceptionally challenging when those relationships are still unresolved or have been particularly painful.

One thing I can say for certain, from working for over 20 years with thousands of people from every conceivable walk of life, is that everyone we meet in this lifetime has an important role to play in our precious journey of evolution in this dimension. I've come to understand that there are absolutely no exceptions to this spiritual truth.

In this chapter, we'll be working with the flesh-and-blood lineages you've been born into and the ancestral patterns you've inherited in this lifetime. Alchemizing and healing the legacy of your ancestors is foundational for manifesting your True Essence.

Ancestral DNA

Our birth family provides the perfect container for us to clear karma and learn the lessons our soul needs in order to evolve.

Everyone we meet in this lifetime has an important role to play in our precious journey of evolution in this dimension. There are absolutely no exceptions to this spiritual truth.

Sometimes we have an affinity with certain family members and feel we've known them before. Alternatively, we might not recognize anyone at all. Do you feel as if you've literally just dropped down from a different planet? Well, you probably have! You'll be here on a specific mission to help your ancestral line move forward.

I'm amazed at how many of us know very little or nothing at all about our ancestral histories. Very occasionally, I will meet someone who is familiar with an entire family tree reaching back hundreds of years. But most times when I'm working on the ancestral piece of the healing jigsaw puzzle, I'm met with, 'My parents don't talk about that side of the family,' which can indicate estrangement, family secrets or a parent not choosing to share parts of their life due to a sense of shame or a fear of being judged.

Other people have grandparents who featured strongly in their lives, but they know nothing of their great-grandparents or the generations that preceded them. Or fragmented stories about grandparents or great-grandparents might be recalled, but they are hazy and obscure.

Put simply, I have found in my work that our parents, grandparents, great-grandparents and all of those that came before them live on through us. Our emotions, mental health and overall sense of vitality, happiness and wellbeing are greatly affected by their legacy.

Connecting with our family lines activates our ancestral DNA and allows us to reclaim the blessings of our lineage. As the African saying goes, 'We stand on their shoulders.' They form the bedrock of who we are.

Create an Altar Dedicated to the Ancestors

Many cultures have shrines in their homes to their ancestral family in the light. To honour and reconnect with your own ancestors, create an altar to them with pictures of relatives who are in spirit and those who are alive in this world now.

Light candles, add flowers and things that you know they might like or have liked in their lives as offerings of love and connection.

Create an Artwork

Another wonderful way to feel the energy of lost generations is to create an artwork or visual of the line of women and men on both sides.

Take the side you are alchemizing and focus on the shape of a person to represent them. You don't need to know anything about them for this work. Gift them with what you feel they need. Pay attention to the images that drop into your heart.

This is what happened when Tringa tried this:

I had been enjoying a period of good physical and mental health when suddenly my sister was diagnosed with cancer. This prompted me to return to Kosovo to support her, where I also reconnected with many family members. However, staying there became challenging, as I found myself absorbing my sister's energy and the collective pain and trauma present in our family, particularly among the women. As time passed, I found myself overwhelmed by the negative energy.

Upon returning to London, I began feeling physically unwell and emotionally distressed. Despite my usual ability to understand my emotions, I felt lost and overwhelmed, experiencing panic attacks, bouts of crying and intrusive dark thoughts. It seemed as though I was unable to regain control of my emotions, which left me physically exhausted and unable to function normally.

Eventually, during a one-on-one session with Estelle, she recognized that some ancestral trauma had been triggered within me. This related to the absence of emotional maternal support and experiences of death within the women in my family. This revelation helped validate my feelings and shed light on the source of my distress.

When Estelle encouraged me to channel for my family, I found myself completely blocked, unable to articulate my thoughts, overwhelmed by a profound sense of emptiness in my chest. It was then that Estelle suggested I had been chosen to break this cycle of trauma and pave a new path for my family lineage.

She instructed me to return home and channel for my family by sketching the women from our lineage, beginning with my grandmother, and providing each with what they needed. Initially, it seemed like an overwhelming task given the depth of trauma in my family, the many women and my own exhaustion. But I cleared the room and invoked the assistance of angels, ancestors and spirit guides to aid me in this endeavour.

As I sketched each woman from my family, I found myself receiving profound insights and guidance. Notably, for one of my aunts, I envisioned young girls surrounding her, and the word 'daughter' emerged. It was only later that my mother revealed that my aunt had longed for daughters for years, but had been unable to have any.

Over the following hours, I tended to each of the women, providing what was needed, whether it be flowers, bright clothing, companionship, laughter or joy – elements that were often lacking in our upbringing. It formed a harmonious circle, bringing a sense of healing as each received what they had longed for. Through this process, I began to notice recurring patterns between mothers and daughters, as well as the types of men they chose to marry.

As the days passed, I found myself gradually feeling better, as if my energy was being restored, returning me to my former self. And while I cannot definitively attribute it to the healing work, it felt miraculous when my sister went into remission.

Tringa

Intergenerational Trauma

Recent research in the field of epigenetics has proven that psychological damage is passed down through DNA as intergenerational trauma.

Kerry Ressler, a neurobiologist and psychiatrist at Emory University in Atlanta, Georgia, had been working in inner cities and seen cycles of addiction, illness and other problems in parents and their children.

'There are a lot of anecdotes to suggest that there's intergenerational transfer of risk,' he said, 'and that it's hard to break that cycle.'

He became interested in epigenetic inheritance, which is how trauma is transferred through DNA, and found that the expression of our genes can change.

Our bodies add or remove 'chemical tags', turning genes on or off as a way of adapting to the environment. So, if our ancestors were subject to neglect or abuse in their homes or had to adapt to extreme periods of hardship, like war, slavery, genocide, famine, sexual violence or natural disasters, their genes would respond accordingly. So, we inherit DNA that has adapted to conditions we have personally never known. Those experiences are in the fibre of our physical bodies. We absolutely inherit our ancestors' trauma.

Whatever our family circumstances, we are an integral part of a long, ever-evolving story. When we decide to liberate ourselves from the destructive burden of unprocessed ancestral DNA and take responsibility for our family lines, we step into our own power, authority and sovereignty and live our best life.

Healing the Ancestors

Transmuting the trauma, wounds and patterns that have been passed down to us through our maternal and paternal bloodlines creates enduring shifts and a powerful dissolving of energetic blocks.

This healing can shift patterns of 'poor health' like cancer, heart disease, high blood pressure, diabetes, arthritis, depression and anxiety. There's great alchemical power in recognizing the pain that you've been unconsciously identifying with and carrying for your family. The healing comes from acknowledging that it doesn't belong to you.

It's not that you abandon your family – quite the contrary! Healing the unhealed stories of our ancestors is an extraordinary privilege, and the entire family line comes along for the ride. Each soul in spirit gets to benefit from this vibrational upgrade. All past, present and future generations will feel the love and the momentous power and dedication of this work.

Our intention here is to facilitate the restoration of our entire lineage to full physical, emotional and spiritual wellness and alignment.

•••

We have three types of ancestors in our family lines: those who expressed and embodied their gifts; those who didn't; and those who abused their power.

Honouring the ancestors who fulfilled their life purpose and existed in harmony with the universal laws unlocks their potent positive energy in our cells and energy field. When we connect with them, they can help us with our struggles, endeavours, hopes, dreams and healing. They stand with us as benevolent guardians in all that we do.

But if our ancestors experienced bleak, hostile or inhumane environments and were unable to step into their true authority or power, their trauma will be trapped in the ancestral line and our energy field. We need to connect with these ancestors to acknowledge their sacrifices and suffering. Witnessing their remarkable fortitude and resilience in the face of adversity will put the angst and torment of that lifetime to rest.

In offering these ancestors healing, we also heal ourselves. We clear the inherited blocks of fear, shame, self-loathing, rage, frustration and hopelessness from our lineage and no longer repeat the patterns that keep us stagnant. These include imposter syndrome, poverty consciousness, thinking small and living in scarcity, lack and fear.

We also activate the untapped qualities and gifts that these ancestors couldn't express in their own lives but have still handed down to us as seeds of potential. Imagine if Leonardo da Vinci had never had the opportunity to hold a paintbrush. All of that creativity would still have existed in him, but would have remained unrealized in his lifetime. We all possess latent gifts and can harness them through this process.

We may also have ancestors who chose to exist out of alignment or integrity. Establishing a spiritual link with these souls liberates us at a cellular level from their wrongdoings, dysfunctional behaviour or acts of malice. We simply wrap our cloak of compassion around them and set them free.

We can also heal these wounds if we are adopted and don't know our birth family, because our ancestral records are still held within us.

We have all chosen this time to incarnate on the planet and each of us has an innate ability to release the shadowy patterns and baggage of those who came before us. We were born to be the mystical alchemists and master healers for our entire lineage. We're collectively clearing humanity's karma for an awakening that is long overdue.

•••

Some of our ancestors already form part of our family in the light, that crack team of spiritual helpers that includes our guardian angels and pets who have passed over. These ancestors have our back and will mostly originate from our more immediate family, so great-grandparents, grandparents, mothers, fathers, brothers, sisters and any children who have passed before us.

I recently facilitated an Embodied-Heart™ ancestral workshop and at the end of the session two women were waiting to talk to me. They were cousins and very excited because during the meditation they'd had the same vision of three family members surrounding them. One of the women clearly recognized her mother and her cousin's father in the group. The other woman said she'd seen the beings, but hadn't been able to identify them. She complained of not having had any sense of her mother since she'd passed over three years before.

I could immediately sense her mother close by and received the message that her unprocessed grief was blocking any discernible communication. This doesn't happen all the time, but in certain cases grief can leave us in a frozen state that blocks the channels of communication. This is one of the reasons why tending to our grief and transmuting the energy of the emotional heart is so important.

One of the most wonderful outcomes of developing our intuition and truly connecting with our benevolent ancestors and our light family is that we never feel alone again. If you could just get a glimpse of how close they are to us! These guys are practically stuck to our sides like glue, and if we nurture our relationships with them by meditating, creating sacred space and developing our ESP and intuition, they will show up more and more with signs, synchronicities and guidance for us.

This very special squad will offer us protection and support and remain around us for our whole lives.

I have found over the years that 'light squad' family members like to arrive in my sessions after my client and I have dropped into the heart space. The mystical heart space is free of the noise of the mind and the pain of the emotional heart, so it's a space of pure connection to Spirit. These light-family souls arrive with significant words, images or messages that guide the session, but essentially they just long to wrap us in a cocoon of love.

•••

Let's think about our inherited patterns now and drill down into how they are impacting our bliss and our freedom today...

This is a good moment to add another tool for self-regulation and self-care. Take yourself into nature for the next exercise, and take your journal and a pen with you.

Exploring the Natural World

This work is bringing you into a deeper relationship with yourself, the people around you and also the Earth itself. So, take some time to get out into nature and explore and strengthen your relationship with the Great Mother.

If you can't get outside of town, find a park, a green space or a garden and spend time noticing the small details and beauty of the natural world around you. Find five things that you have noticed and journal about them.

The stillness of nature helps us practise mindfulness and being in the present moment, which reduces anxiety, blood pressure and the production of stress hormones. A recent scientific study has found that nature has the power to rewire the brain's neural pathways, which is a massive support for us during the True Essence Process as we begin to peel back the layers and heal at our core. It also allows our prefrontal cortex, which is responsible for attention and decision-making, to rest and recharge.

Nature is medicine. The water cleanses, the sun nourishes, the wind whispers, the trees teach, the plants heal, the moon inspires, the flowers enchant. When you are looking for alignment and inner nourishment, find a place in the arms of nature.

Now, looking at your life, consider the areas of: family, love, work, money, health and wellbeing. For each of these areas, list the patterns that you recognize have been handed down to you through your family line.

Journal Prompts

Here are a few ideas to think about:

* Can you identify any cycles of addiction, like alcohol, drug, gambling, food, sex, love or work, handed down from your mother's or father's families? Are you continuing these patterns in your own life?

* Did you witness any infidelity/manipulation/conflict aversion growing up? Does this play out in your relationships today?

* Did either side of your family experience or obsess about not having enough? Was there poverty, scarcity, bad luck, the fear of losing wealth, a limited belief in the possibility of abundance or material success? Were there problems with inheritance or losing out?

* Are you repeating dysfunctional patterns of communication like passive aggressive or aggressive tantrums, moods and avoidant behaviours like putting down the phone or storming out of the room?

* Are you recreating a mother or father wound or a sibling rivalry with your children?

* Can you identify any other patterns that may have been handed down to you, like envy, lying, secrecy, isolation or control?

Once you are aware of these patterns, you have the opportunity to break the cycle by reframing damaging stories told to you as a child with positive self-talk, affirmations and soul activism, which involves being actively engaged and present with your patterns as they are happening in real time and stepping into your compassionate adult in the moment.

•••

Take my father's story. A year before he passed away in 2019, I sat down with him on his balcony in Barbados, with the southeastern Caribbean Sea on one side and the Atlantic on the other. Set neatly on a hill in the parish of St Michael, Bridgetown, this was a house that he had practically built by himself over many years of squirrelling his pennies away whilst working in England.

We sat above the fruit trees that he'd proudly planted some decades before – mango, orange and breadfruit. We both stared quietly out over Bridgetown harbour and the expanse of glistening blue ocean to a large cruise ship on the horizon, and I was struck by how frail and sad he was. I felt I was losing him. His health, memory and morale had deteriorated dramatically during the previous year as a result of a series of falls.

After a few moments of gentle silence, he began to tell me about how he had first left his beloved Barbados 63 years before to make something of himself in England. I had heard the story many times over the years, but that day I knew somewhere deep inside that I might not hear it again. So I scribbled down some notes, cherishing the words in a new way.

In 1948, the *Empire Windrush* delivered the first 500 Caribbeans from all over the West Indies to work and settle in the UK. They had been recruited by the British government to help the country fill employment vacancies and recover economically after the Second World War. These bright young men and women arrived full of hope to work for the Royal Mail, National Health Service and London Transport. They had high expectations of their new lives. The United Kingdom was the motherland, after all. They had been taught for four centuries that it was the epicentre of everything worthwhile.

Four years later, my adventurous 19-year-old father was inspired to follow those first intrepid immigrants. Like his father before him, he played the saxophone in the police band, and he supplemented his income by putting on little magic shows in schools to save up to buy his ticket.

He remembers his mother waving a tearful farewell at the edge of the dock in Bridgetown as he boarded a ship that would take him to Cannes in the south of France. Not speaking a word of French, he managed to catch a train to Paris and eventually a ferry across the Channel to Dover. He turned up in London alone and knowing no one.

I marvel at this story and at the fortitude, bravery, tenacity and faith of that first wave of Caribbean pioneers. Not only did my father survive, but in his way he thrived. He was a virtuoso musician who touched souls and opened hearts with the music that poured through him. There was something eternally joyful and optimistic in his spirit. He had a great sense of humour and his infectious smile could light up a room from end to end.

I loved him very much and felt loved by him too. And in the spirit of dialectical truth, where two opposing truths can sit side by side and both be true at the same time, he also handed down the intergenerational wound of the absent father to me. Broken family systems are symptomatic of the trauma of the trans-Atlantic slave trade and continue to affect everyone who is part of the African diaspora.

This intergenerational trauma left me feeling deeply unsupported, angry, abandoned and ultimately unloved by the masculine. This was a father wound that had been handed down by the men in my father's family.

Educators, teachers and musicians had featured on both his maternal and paternal sides. But the men had also been heavy drinkers, and over the years I heard many stories of how they would think nothing of drinking large tumblers of rum every night.

My grandfather died suddenly when my dad was 13, and being the eldest of seven siblings, he immediately stepped into the breach. With no adequate time to grieve, he responded as men were expected to at that time: suppressing his feelings and doing his best to become the man of the house. Whilst in truth he was largely dazed and ill-equipped for the role.

Interestingly, when my mother and father literally collided coming out of an audition for the sixties cult play *Hair*, they had a lot in common. And beneath the merry chit-chat of their first meeting were two experiences that recognized each other. They both had alcoholic fathers and an absent father wound, which is prevalent in relationships where ancestral wounding remains unaddressed. We trauma bond unconsciously around the stories we carry in our DNA. The energy of these stories is ours to transmute.

My work as the steward of my ancestral line is to make sure that I don't pass down the wound of the absent father to my son. This doesn't mean you don't separate or divorce if you need to, but if this does happen, you build the interpersonal bridge to transmute painful emotions in the moment so they aren't internalized as a belief that undermines the Divine Masculine within. This is about breaking the cycle of fathers who are the unloved sons of unloved sons and restoring self-esteem, love, pride, respect and courage in the masculine.

Meeting the Ancestors

If we can encourage our ancestors to emerge from the shadows of our unconscious and our energy field, we can begin the work of repairing and reprogramming our ancestral DNA and experience peace at a deep cellular level.

The healing and honouring of your ancestors is a fundamental step on the path to reconnecting with your True Essence.

Circle of Life Meditation

This is a moment in time when you are going to meet your ancestors in the inter-dimensional space that surrounds us in the unseen world. Know that you are already the healer, pattern-breaker, alchemist and guide for all those who came before you.

Find a comfortable space to create sacred space. Include four objects to represent the elements of Earth, Air, Fire and Water. We are surrounded by these elements, with the earth under our feet, the air that we breathe, the fire of the sun and the water of the oceans, rivers and streams. These elements sustain all life on Earth, so it makes sense to honour them.

So, bring a crystal or stone into your space for Earth, and burn incense, sage or a resin like frankincense or myrrh on charcoal for Air. Use blessed or holy water, rainwater or a seashell for Water, and light a candle in honour of your ancestors to represent the element of Fire.

Check in with how grounded you are feeling. Spend more time grounding if you need to by imagining roots growing down deep into the earth from your base chakra.

Call in your compassionate adult and say out loud:

> *'In this moment I am creating a safe sacred container*
> *for the rightful return of all those from my ancestral*
> *lineage, known and unknown, to facilitate a return*
> *to wholeness, grace and true divinity.'*

Place your hands in the middle of your chest and become aware of your breath. Over the course of five deep breaths you are going to drop into the three chambers of your heart.

Begin with becoming aware of your physical heart.

Then breathe into your emotional heart and notice how you are feeling.

Then, on the fifth breath, gently open the door to your mystical heart and step across the boundary from the darkness into the light.

Imagine you are sitting in a clearing surrounded by very ancient trees. You are sitting cross-legged, enjoying the heat of a powerful fire that is burning in the centre of the circle.

A canopy of stars is suspended above you in a clear, midnight-blue sky. Notice the moon. Is it waning or waxing, Full Moon or crescent, or is it a New Moon and the sky is dark?

Trust the ears and eyes of your heart-mind.

Feel a soft, cool breeze touch your cheek as it cleanses the clearing, rustling gently through the leaves.

Visualize the flames of the fire for a moment, then close your eyes and take some long deep breaths into their warmth. This is an image that is stored within our cellular memory, because at some point in all our histories our ancestors have sat around a fire just like this one, in a circle, under the stars.

Your ancestors' frequency is held within your own cells and energetic field. Invite them to step forward and join you by saying these words, either out loud or in your heart:

'I call upon my ancestors from both my maternal
and paternal lines to be here now.

Step forward, come and warm your hands at my fire.
Join me here at the crossroads, in this timeline, to
begin our process of healing and transformation.

I invite you all to share your story to assist the
clearing of any patterns, burdens or curses that are
blocking the evolution of our ancestral line.

Be here now, be here now, be here now.

And so it is. Blessed Be/Amen/Ase.'

Trust that your ancestors have been waiting for this opportunity to meet you since the beginning of time.

Repeat the invitation like a mantra.

Notice figures stepping out from the shadows into the light. Your ancestors are joining you, taking their rightful place, one by one, or in twos and threes, in your sacred circle. It's okay if you don't see their faces or form, just trust their energy.

The clearing expands as more and more of your ancestors join you.

Some of your ancestors will stop and face you. They will communicate an emotion, an image or a story to you. Be open to asking them questions to help them communicate more with you.

You can also ask the good ancestors to present themselves to help you transmute the energy of the line.

Visualize your heart radiating a frequency of compassion and grace. Imagine this frequency as a combination of golden and green light. Send it like a wave to the heart of each ancestor and see their hearts activate and connect with one another. Know that you are healing all of the deep spiritual, psychological and physical fractures and wounds with your web of light and love.

Thank them for their lives and contribution to your life and this moment.

And so it is...

Gently open your eyes and journal about what has been revealed to you.

Check in with your heart and return to the Circle of Life meditation for as long as you need to. Spend time meeting different ancestors, building relationships with your ancestral guardians and infusing your kin with divine light. Remember that you're the conduit for this meaningful work.

Releasing the Ancestors

As you break the shackles that have held your ancestors hostage, separated from the beauty of their own inner gold, you're also embodying profound compassion for different aspects of yourself. This is Love in action, as Sarah experienced when she released the women in her family from the repression of the toxic masculine and healed her inner child at the same time...

I went to work with Estelle having walked away from 10 long years in the finance industry and recovered from drug and alcohol abuse, as well as a later mastectomy and reconstruction following a genetic mutation diagnosis. I was tired, timid and, I think, searching for something.

I believed that my 'block' was about bodily healing and walking away from toxic people, including men, and I wanted to understand why I believed that love was perhaps never going to come my way. Having originally trained as an actress, I knew my creative artist was there, but locked deep in a box. I also knew she wanted to get out, but I was emotionally incapable of letting her emerge.

In the first session, Estelle placed healing stones on my body and held my hand, and the tears came hard and fast and were about none of the above, to my surprise. It was raw, desperate grief. My grandparents had died years before, and had been the great loves of my life, my grandmother in particular. Following their death, I had been embroiled in a dark world of cocaine abuse and consequently my grief had never been able to just be.

This session started something. Estelle suggested the Love Retreat to me and a few weeks later we were there.

When it came to the big healing day, I felt the space was extremely charged and I didn't know what to expect, but I trusted Estelle and knew this space was safe.

I lay down and the other women came in and formed a circle around me. My eyes were closed. What I remember is that my body started to shake hard and sweat formed on my hands and feet. I had an experience that I think was similar to when people say, 'My life flashed before my eyes.' There was a lot of dark fog and it was visceral and desperate. I started to shout, 'Go away!'

After a few minutes I remember Estelle saying, 'If there is more to release, then do it.'

I was exhausted, but it occurred to me that it wasn't just about me. My grandmother was there, and her mother, and her mother, and I had a clear image of leading an army of women into battle, an army of my women, and then I pushed on and released this heavy darkness, this toxic web entangling me.

Afterwards, my body was so damp, but something had gone. I felt lighter and like my inner child was somehow smiling at me.

It was only the next day, in the final sharing circle, that I shared what had occurred to me in that moment: that it was about my women and the toxic masculine that we had endured and accepted, and therefore carried. My weight, my darkness, my obstacles and my low self-worth were inherited trauma...

Following the retreat, my life has been different. I've started a new job on my terms, I've reconnected with the theatrical arts and I'm nearly always involved in performance again. Within a year, my person walked into my life and now we live together and enjoy nature and all the beautiful things in life. I am seen and I am loved. I exercise the power of 'no'; I know my worth and my boundaries. I keep no toxic relationships or company that does not serve me. I enjoy my family more. I have forgiven the former me who was lost and vibrating in negative spaces.

On tough days, I connect with nature and take a journal out with me. I think about my women and know I have so much to be grateful for. Everything is better and brighter because I gave in, I listened to my heart and I went into battle in Somerset.

Sarah

One of the most wonderful outcomes
of developing our intuition and truly
connecting with our benevolent
ancestors and our light family is
that we never feel alone again.

Often, when we have been the family scapegoat, alienated or completely misunderstood, or alternatively have been the glue within the family dynamic, part of our karma is to release the ancestors on both sides of our family lines.

Here is another example of the potential of ancestral healing, this time based on Family Constellation Therapy, which was developed by German psychotherapist Bert Hellinger. This involves a group of people coming together and each assuming the role of a different family member. The feelings, thoughts and energy of that person are channelled by whoever is playing them, and this is effective whether that family member is alive or has already passed over.

The work originated from the 16 years that Hellinger spent in South Africa around Zulu shaman priests. Communication with and reverence for the Amadlozi, or ancestral spirits, is an intrinsic part of traditional African life. They are the good ancestors who provide us with protection and guidance and can help us clear blocks in all areas of life – spiritual, physical and material.

Hellinger witnessed many shamanic ceremonies, including a particular ritual that was used to contact deceased relatives to clear the family line. I use a variation of this in my work, channelling the inter-dimensional slipstream of the Divine too...

Through role-play and tapping into the mystical quantum field of the past with Estelle in a family constellation, I discovered the origins of the toxic family dynamics that had been passed down generationally. This was difficult for me, as many of the key people who had the most impact on my life have transitioned, so there was also an element of guilt for revisiting their traumas and revealing their worst aspects in a group environment. I trusted the group, though, and everyone understood that we were there not to blame or accuse but to heal.

When the role-play started, I asked my dad why he had showed so much hatred towards me and my immediate family. And why I felt that he had such a strong dislike of women in particular. He admitted that he did, but didn't know why.

Estelle intuitively felt that it had something to do with my grandma, so brought her in. The lady who was playing my grandmother immediately had chills and described her energy as uncaring and cold. I remembered that there were many times when my grandma had exhibited those characteristics, as much as I wanted to remember her as a gentle and caring woman.

So I learned that my dad's unloving relationship with his mother meant he developed a deep mistrust of women. I felt a lot of compassion for him in that moment. I felt that he carried that feeling of never being properly loved throughout his life and that was why he rejected any emotional intimacy with anyone. He rejected his children because he, too, was rejected.

We then went deeper and tried to find the root of this toxicity in my family line. Other members of the group played my ancestors. They described how their energy felt cold, unemotional and almost a bit ruthless. It started with two ancestors who harboured the absolute worst elements of the toxic masculine and feminine. This felt familiar – I had felt this darkness in my wider family for as long as I could remember.

I selected two individuals in the group to embody Divine Masculine and Feminine qualities to psychically neutralize the toxic polarities.

During the constellation, I also stood up to my father and asserted myself in the face of the abusive male power. At first I found this really difficult. Then I selected two individuals to stand behind me as representations of the Divine Masculine and Feminine. I then selected other group members to play the females in my family who had also suffered. This gave me the strength to speak up for myself and tell my dad that his behaviours were unacceptable and that he needed to back off. I felt as if I was standing up for all women everywhere. It was a very powerful moment. My dad apologized to me and knew that he could have done better. I embraced him and his energy softened.

Once the exercise was over, I felt I had received a huge revelation about my ancestral history. So many times in my life I had actually asked myself why the energy in my family felt so brutal, so punishing. Now I understand why and my role in breaking the cycle.

On reflection, what this exercise showed me most of all was the power of the Divine Masculine and Feminine – how it is so needed in the world and might just be the cure for many of our traumas.

Annisa

Annisa unearthed and transformed a toxic legacy that had been handed down for generations on her paternal side. She bravely neutralized this pattern with firm intention and love, restoring a sense of divinity to the family line in this family constellation. By standing up to her father's abuse, she was protecting and healing her inner child, embodying her power and authority and finding her adult voice in the process.

She also felt a new sense of compassion for her father in this session. She gained an eagle-eye perspective on his trauma and could begin to forgive him.

Annisa had reached the pivotal moment in the healing of her emotional heart where she was organically cultivating a state of grace within. She had taken her first steps onto the bridge to the mystic heart and was closer to returning to wholeness, to her True Essence.

CHAPTER 8

Grace Is the Bridge

*'I do not at all understand
the mystery of grace –
only that it meets us where we are but does
not leave us where it found us.'*
ANNE LAMOTT

Changes have been happening inside you throughout this process of opening the heart. Perhaps they were inspired by your sacred encounters with the Divine Feminine, your inner child or ancestors. Throughout this experience of softening and dismantling your barriers to love and illuminating more of your Shadow, you may have found you have been dreaming more, or scattered and forgotten memories could be emerging from your unconscious.

Have you recognized parts of yourself in the stories you've read, or found guidance, an image or a revelation dropping into your consciousness through the journalling exercises or meditations and visualizations that you've been doing?

Often we have our 'Aha!' breakthroughs and understand the work more when we're going about the normal business of our daily lives – at the gym, walking the dog, making meals or travelling to work. In these seemingly innocuous moments, our mind can drift back to an idea, feeling or practice and it will land in our psyche a little differently than before and subsequently make more sense to us.

So, the inner alchemy will be well under way now, which means it's time to leave the emotional heart and enter the chamber of the mystic heart. The time has come to cross the bridge...

•••

A bridge is always a place of transition, and today we're symbolically crossing from one state of being to another one.

When we cross this sacred bridge, we begin to gently integrate everything that we've understood with our mind and experienced in our physical body and emotional heart on this journey so far. This is also where we'll meet our last holy companion. Perhaps you've encountered her before. She is the sister of compassion, and goes by the name of Grace...

In ancient Greece, Grace was honoured as a goddess of fertility and associated with beauty, creativity and charm. Originally she was also referred to as a 'pleasing' or 'charming' field or garden, and her three aspects, known as the Three Graces – Aglaia (Brightness), Euphrosyne (Joyfulness) and Thalia (Bloom) – would fill the land with her abundance. As we cross the bridge, Grace fills our pockets with special gifts and wisdom so that when we reach the garden of our mystic heart, the seeds of our future can be planted in fruitful soil. They are destined to joyfully grow and bloom, watered with the power of Love...

'The heart is like a candle,
longing to be lit.
Torn from the Beloved,
it yearns to be whole again,
but you have to bear the pain.
You cannot learn about love.
Love appears on the wings of grace.'
RUMI

Grace invites us to trust the abundance of the universe and surrender to its divine timing and the magical future that we will soon be co-creating with it. She will teach you about humility and, most importantly, invite you to forgive, accept and release anything else that could be holding you back from embracing your unique magic and power in this moment.

Bring both hands to your heart chakra, close your eyes and take five deep heart-embodied breaths.

Visualize walking onto a bridge. Notice your feet and the precious steps that you are taking from your emotional heart back home to your mystic heart and True Essence. These are solid, slow and mindful steps that are bringing you back into the arms of Love.

Notice a figure standing at the midpoint of the bridge, beckoning you on. This is Grace, one of your greatest cheerleaders. She is so happy to finally see your face. Observe her robes and beautiful aura shimmering in the light of this new day. They are fashioned from the luminous qualities of humility, forgiveness, acceptance, surrender and gratitude.

As we cross this bridge together, we cultivate our own state of grace within, by exploring some of her divine attributes.

Forgiveness and Acceptance

The Chinese sage and philosopher Confucius, writing 2,500 years ago, said, 'Humility is the foundation of all virtues.' Modern thinking misunderstands the importance of humility. Being humble doesn't mean we're timid or lacking in confidence. Humility is vital for our soul's evolution to help us stay open and in our heart. But what I've found from working with thousands of different people from all walks of life is that whilst humility is the foundation, it's forgiveness that brings the fire and kick-starts our relationship with Grace. When we commit to forgiveness at some level, everything else falls effortlessly into place.

If you spend a few moments thinking back through your life, you'll remember times when it's been easy to forgive and move on and other experiences that you have stuffed away but are still holding on to right now. At some point on every healing journey, there's invariably someone to forgive or something that requires us to accept it.

Forgiveness and acceptance are like different currents of the same soft but purposeful wind that circles underneath our wings to help us take flight. These are the wings that you've been lovingly growing throughout this process of inner alchemy.

> *'Observational studies, and even some randomized trials,*
> *suggest that forgiveness is associated with lower levels of*
> *depression, anxiety, and hostility; reduced substance abuse;*
> *higher self-esteem; and greater life satisfaction.*
> *Yet, forgiving people is not always easy.'*
> TYLER VANDERWEELE, *'THE POWER OF FORGIVENESS'*

On my own journey, as I faced and tended to my Shadow, inner child, shame and ancestors, I slowly nurtured my inner state of grace. I reparented my younger self over the years, and, like Annisa, my compassionate adult put my parents' stories into an ancestral and psychological framework. This gifted me with a benevolent eagle's perspective on the behaviour and choices that had impacted me so heavily growing up. Both parents had recycled patterns of trauma and suffering because they lacked the appropriate tools or resources to respond to life in any other way at the time.

One morning during a meditation I visualized them as children and was struck by their innocence and sweetness. I found myself wrapping their younger selves in love and embracing them tenderly in the soft creases of my heart. The Divine Feminine and the slipstream of compassion helped me to forgive them.

Finally, I could honour the resilience and courage my parents had embodied throughout their lives to survive their own stories. I felt immensely grateful for the experiences and soul lessons of my childhood, as a deep sense of freedom and peace began to settle into my emotional heart. I was also deeply grateful to my parents for giving me the gift of life. From a state of grace, I accepted my mother and father for who they were – perfectly imperfect souls on the planet, trying to make their way back home like everyone else.

Uncovering

Sometimes clients arrive in denial about past trauma, and we spend time in the uncovering stage before we reach the forgiveness stage. Bullying at school or within friendship groups is a common experience that people deny or minimize.

When we're in denial of our trauma, we're naturally disconnected from the need to forgive. But there are huge benefits when that repressed pain is acknowledged.

The uncovering stage inevitably leads to an outpouring of grief and then at the right time we can approach the idea of forgiveness. This is where we get to work with our healed and healing adult and our developing state of grace to pour compassion into the places where we feel the greatest pain.

The Power of Forgiveness

There have been thousands of scientific studies over the last 25 years investigating the phenomenon of forgiveness and its impact on mind, body and spirit. Scientists in America observed 1,800 people for The REACH Forgiveness programme and found something truly remarkable about the nature of forgiveness and how it can change you forever. They noted that 'merely dwelling' on the benefits of forgiveness for around 10 minutes actually inspired more forgiveness in the participants.

So, just thinking about forgiveness for 10 minutes a day has the power to facilitate the restoration of our inner serenity. That's pretty good news!

> 'Not only does forgiveness benefit relationships at home, work, socially, and societally, but it can also lower our cortisol, which is a primary stress hormone contributing to adrenal exhaustion and burn-out. Soon after experiencing forgiveness, our heart-rate variability increases, which means we can self-soothe more easily and we release more of the "love hormone," oxytocin, which facilitates feelings of connection, trust, happiness, and empathy.'
>
> EVERETT L. WORTHINGTON, JR, GREATER GOOD MAGAZINE

When we don't forgive, emotions like bitterness, resentment, hatred and corrosive anger get stuck inside our emotional body and these unprocessed emotions lead to exhaustion, stress, anxiety and low-level depression.

One of the things that can really get in the way of healing is when we get stuck in the toxic blame loop. This loop is our ego's response to being harmed by others and the natural sense of injustice that results from this harm. We get completely preoccupied by a need for the perpetrator to apologize and acknowledge their wrongdoing. It's a hard loop to break, because we're convinced that we can't move on without this external validation.

Alternatively, the idea of any interaction with the perpetrator might feel overwhelming. This is especially true if we believe they might try to gaslight our truth and that what we say will fall on deaf ears. I often hear: 'What's the point?'

The point of this process is that your healing doesn't rely on anyone else, it's on *your* terms, and most importantly, reconciliation is not necessary for resolution. So, whilst you can choose to work through any hurt or injury and repair a damaged relationship if that serves you, it's not necessary for closure. The keys to your peace are in *your* hands. *You* have the power now.

> '*Though I was unaware of it at the time, that simple*
> *act of forgiveness was the beginning of an entirely*
> *new level of experiencing life for me.*'
> **WAYNE DYER**

And remember, forgiveness doesn't equate to denying the seriousness of what happened to you. We don't forget, excuse, condone or justify wrongdoing, but we don't need to air our grievances in person or wait for others to take accountability for their actions to move on.

Forgiveness is a radical gesture of self-love and profoundly transformational, as Tringa discovered at a True Essence workshop...

> After a decade of talking therapy, I found myself entrenched in bitterness and estrangement from my father, a rift born of the weight of unresolved grievances from the past. The mere thought of forgiveness seemed inconceivable, as the wounds ran deep and the scars remained fresh. Yet, during a weekend of working with the heart, something extraordinary unfolded – an encounter that felt nothing short of divine intervention.

> Sitting among the group, one of the women shared her story of forgiving the abuse that she had been subjected to as a child. Her willingness to release resentment left me dumbfounded. How could she possibly pardon such a substantial wrongdoing? I pondered. The concept of forgiveness had always seemed beyond reach for me until that moment.

> Witnessing her capacity to forgive sparked a revelation within me: if she could extend forgiveness in such circumstances, then surely I could do the same for my father. In that instant, a deep understanding swept over me, as though an intangible force had delicately steered my heart towards the path of forgiveness. It occurred in a mere instant – suddenly, I forgave, and a sense of liberation washed over me.

> With newfound clarity, I reached out to my father the following day, embarking on a journey to mend fractured ties. As we engaged in heartfelt conversation, the walls of resentment crumbled, paving the way for genuine understanding and reconciliation.

When we choose to forgive, we
restore our psychic wellbeing
and transmute heavy feelings
and emotions into gold.

Over a year has passed since that pivotal moment, and I now cherish a beautiful relationship with my father. Through the transformative power of forgiveness, I have liberated myself from the shackles of resentment and embraced a future defined by love and healing.

Tringa

Forgiving Yourself

One of the greatest challenges I witness in sessions is when we need to forgive and accept *ourselves* for perceived mistakes. It's especially difficult to forgive ourselves for the times we've abandoned ourselves, like putting ourselves in dangerous situations or tolerating abusive relationships for too long.

Self-forgiveness challenges the judgemental and perfectionist inner critic that likes to punish us. We're invited to offer kindness and love to ourselves instead, which can feel very unfamiliar.

In these instances, it's important to give yourself as much time as you need. The process of inner resolution is different for everyone, and it doesn't happen overnight. If you discover that there are a few layers to work through, have patience. This part of your healing story may be ongoing for some time. This isn't a competition. There are no top marks for finishing first or ticking all the boxes.

If the idea of forgiveness is in your awareness, it's enough. And you're reading these words, so it's more than enough.

Grab your journal and a pen and find a quiet, comfortable place to contemplate forgiveness, acceptance and the holy companion of this chapter, Grace.

Close your eyes and bring yourself into your body and the present moment by taking some deep breaths. Sink into your heart space.

Ask your heart if you're carrying any experiences, known or unknown, that might require forgiveness and acceptance.

Say any names our loud or bring a particular event to mind and notice how your body responds. Perhaps you feel a rush of energy moving through you or experience a tightness in your throat, chest or stomach. You might become tense or agitated and your heart rate could increase.

Reflect on whether you're holding grudges, keeping score, ruminating on how you have been wronged or obsessing over how you can seek revenge.

Do you fantasize about what you would say or do to someone if you had your time with them again?

Are there any traumatic or undermining events from your childhood, teenage years or adult life that you have discounted or minimized?

Write down the situations and events that have happened in your life where you can apply forgiveness and acceptance to yourself.

Think about the different qualities of our holy companion Grace: forgiveness, acceptance, humility and gratitude. Write about each quality and which ones would benefit from increased awareness and practice in your life.

A State of Grace

Remember, developing a state of grace doesn't make you *passive, emotionally by-passy, a doormat or a pushover.* This isn't about bowing your head and shuffling away, dejected and resigned to your lot in life. Rather, this is a spine straight, shoulders back, head held high moment.

There's a distinct difference between surrendering to a situation from a place of powerlessness and accepting a situation from a place of empowerment. And forgiveness is a radically *empowered* choice. When we decide to actively forgive, we're co-creating with the universe.

This co-creation helps us take back the reins of our destiny. Our happiness is now our responsibility.

This happens because when we choose to forgive, we're also:

- recognizing and honouring the pain and harm we suffered in the past

- . naming and validating our own emotions

- choosing to 'give back' the painful legacy of the experience(s) to the perpetrator(s), rather than allowing them to define us

- relinquishing our victim status

- giving ourselves permission to move on.

By releasing the people who have caused us trauma, we focus on our joy rather than our suffering. It's a courageous step, but if you choose to take it now, it will help you acknowledge the pain that you've suffered without having that pain define the rest of your life, as Jules discovered:

For me, to have found forgiveness is also to have found freedom from my trauma. I feel safe within my body, mind and soul. The world seems open and accessible like never before, and it has come from finding compassion and forgiveness.

Yet when I first met Estelle three years ago, I was so terrified, I couldn't speak. I think I only said, 'Hello,' and my name. It had only been 10 days since I'd told my therapist what had happened to me as a child. So, when Estelle held my feet and did a heart meditation, I saw my inner child, my blackened heart, in the internal turmoil I was in. I knew Estelle had seen everything as well, and not having to tell her helped, but I was in such a state of shock. Still, something had unblocked, and I felt I could move forward and possibly even hope to live my life.

A year of some real highs and deep lows followed, all of which were very scary. I was still unable to tell anyone about my past. However, six months later I went on a Love Retreat and over that weekend I opened my heart to myself for the first time, and a lot of self-loathing dissipated and compassion for myself came in.

Eventually, I realized I needed help to release more emotion. I could identify my emotions, but not feel them truly. I met with the first True Essence practitioner group, sat in a room of mostly strangers and told them my story. Then I cried in their arms for hours. It felt like I was crying for 23 years, mourning what my life could have been, who I could have been, the happiness I should have had, the unfairness, the confusion, all of it. I was emotional for days after. So, I spent six weeks practising yoga, feeling into my body and releasing the hurt, grief and sadness.

Since then, there have been issues to work through, but I have been free in a way I never imagined. I have tools to fall back on when things arise, which of course they do. I still have stress and anxiety and I'm working on my inner critic, which is very hard, but I do love myself so much more.

To have found forgiveness and compassion doesn't mean I am validating what happened or have forgotten it, but I have relinquished it. To me, this means I can move forward with my life.

Jules

> *'We must develop and maintain the capacity to forgive. He who is devoid of the power to forgive is devoid of the power to love.'*
> MARTIN LUTHER KING

Forgiveness Ritual

Choose to begin this ritual on a New Moon and complete it two weeks later on the Full Moon. Harness the power of the Earth's natural cycles to help you create sacred space and release what no longer serves you.

Light a candle and call in your family in the light to assist and support this work.

Begin with the heart meditation (*see page 36*). Drop down into your heart space.

Bring your past hurts to mind and notice that they're not in this physical reality.

Recall the perpetrators of the injustices you are carrying and make a list of their names in your journal.

Also list the things you have done to other people and are choosing to forgive yourself for in this moment.

Two weeks later, at the Full Moon, connect with God and your family in the light and hand over all your past injuries and injustices to them...

Refrain from judgement and infuse your being with ripples of love. You can imagine ripples of iridescent pink, gold and blue. Send this energy to all those you are letting go of in this moment. Speak these words out loud...

> *'I give myself permission to be in the present moment, free*
> *of the people and experiences that no longer serve me.*
>
> *I give myself permission to forgive myself. I*
> *release all self-loathing and shame.*
>
> *I purify myself from all those who have*
> *damaged my peace. I release you.*
>
> *I liberate myself in this moment from those*
> *who have hurt me physically, psychologically,*
> *emotionally and spiritually. I release you.*
>
> *I release all transgressions to my mind, body and spirit.*
>
> *I release all feelings of betrayal from my*
> *emotional and physical bodies.*
>
> *I embrace my emancipation and restoration in this moment.*
>
> *At my core I am grace and in this moment I am returning*
> *to a state of embodied grace. At my core I am humility,*
> *love and acceptance. I am grace incarnate and I am*
> *returning to that state of grace, my sacred birthright.*
>
> *And so it is.*
>
> *And so it is.*
>
> *And so it is.*
>
> *Blessed Be/Amen/Ase.'*

There is a soft flow of freedom running through the river of forgiveness, a ribbon of light that pierces the darkness of wrongdoing... Baptize yourself there, in those clear waters.

Anoint yourself with Love.

Give your innocence back to yourself.

Follow the guidance of your heart and repeat at the next Full Moon if necessary.

Write about your experience of the forgiveness ritual in your journal.

Acceptance

Forgiveness and acceptance are intrinsically intertwined. One cannot happen without the other. We can't forgive until we've fully accepted our reality. When we can accept that a situation or person isn't changing and that it isn't our job to change it or them, we can let go. So, walking over the bridge and actively choosing to forgive means you're already accepting that something no longer serves you and it's time to let it go.

Surrender takes acceptance a step further. It ignites the flame of trust within us. Feeling fearful, uncertain or anxious is a clear sign that we're not trusting the universe to hold us safe and deliver on our hopes and dreams. We're relying on our own strength instead of the strength of the Creator.

Trust that little by little what's meant for you will find its way to you. There's no need to chase or force anything. Surrender to the flow and being present in the moment.

Close your eyes now and take yourself back to the bridge. Allow Grace to take you softly by the hand. Her eyes are smiling and radiating unconditional love. She wants you to know that you are loved more than you could ever imagine. Be grateful for it. Gratitude is her parting gift to you...

Gratitude

In offering up our gratitude, we open ourselves to receiving and living in a state of grace. The word 'gratitude' comes from the Latin word *gratia*, which means 'grace', 'graciousness' or 'gratefulness'. Gratitude brings our brain, heart, body and spirit into a state of harmony and optimum wellbeing.

> *'Being so grateful even before you receive – this*
> *is the stuff that creates miracles.'*
> LOUISE HAY

A lot has been written and spoken about gratitude in recent years and you've probably already tried keeping a gratitude journal or have one now. But, like everything we've shared so far, this is a journey through the heart, not through the mind. So, don't think gratitude, feel it. Let it radiate through the channel of your heart that is now healed and healing.

Let it make you feel good. Focusing on what you have rather than what you don't have and counting your blessings wires and fires neural connections for happiness. When we develop a regular gratefulness practice, our brain releases more dopamine and serotonin, the neurotransmitters responsible for feel-good emotions. Feeling grateful also creates better heart coherence and regulates our nervous and immune systems.

Grateful people forgive more, and become less anxious and fearful. They also sleep better and experience less loneliness in their lives.

But what I've noticed over the years is that complex trauma can sometimes eclipse our access to gratitude. Some people just can't see their way through to this type of positive thinking, because gratitude usually touches on the big accomplishments or relationships in our lives. What happens if we don't have any examples of these things to fall back on? Then it's time to look out for the glimmers in your life.

Glimmers

Glimmers are micro-moments of joy that can happen throughout the day. They can be anything from smelling the aroma of good food or the sea on the breeze to listening to birdsong, a baby's giggle or your favourite song on the radio. The term was coined by Deb Dana and Stephen Porges in their book *The Polyvagal Theory in Therapy*.

A young man recently came to see me who was recovering from a severe gambling addiction that had consumed most of his teens and early twenties. He had grown up with an alcoholic mother and an absent and uninterested father. He'd heard about the potential of gratitude, but had drawn a blank when he'd thought about what he could be grateful for. Of course, we think of things like having a roof over our head and food on the table, but he had those things growing up and it had still been a hugely traumatic experience for him.

We discussed the concept of glimmers, and I left him for a few moments to jot down any glimmers he could identify from that day. He wrote down two: 'I woke up and the sun was shining' and 'I have someone to talk to.'

Imagine gratitude as a big magnet.
As you walk through the world, it has
the power to draw good things to you
and manifest miracles in your life.

Fortunately, even identifying one glimmer a day is enough to stimulate the parasympathetic nervous system to create sensations of calm and build neural pathways that will wire the brain for beauty, presence and peace rather than potential threat, crisis and danger. Glimmers are simple and fleeting, but can generate feelings of safety, hope, peace and calm.

Journal Prompts

* If you feel you can't start with a gratefulness diary, begin with a glimmers one instead. Close your eyes and recall a glimmer. Sit with the feeling of that glimmer for at least 10 seconds. Breathe it into your heart and let it bring a smile to your face.

* If you are keeping a gratefulness diary, list all the things that you're grateful for, and also the things that haven't happened yet but you're manifesting right now!

* Engage the magic of your heart by dropping into your heart first and then visualizing a scene from the future as if it has already happened.

* Add this to your daily practice.

You have crossed the bridge. Give thanks to Grace for her love, support, gifts and wisdom.

Now we are crossing the last threshold. We are returning to the garden.

> *'Love cannot be far behind a grateful heart and thankful mind...*
> *These are the true conditions for your homecoming.'*
> **A COURSE IN MIRACLES**

PART III

Returning

'How did the rose ever open its heart
And give to this world all its beauty?
It felt the encouragement of light against its being.
Otherwise, we all remain too frightened.'

HAFIZ

CHAPTER 9

The Garden

*'Listen to your heart. It knows all things, because it came
from the soul of the world and it will one day return there.'*
PAULO COELHO

You have reached the mystic chamber of the heart.

You should feel *so* proud of how far you've come on this journey. Entering
your emotional heart, you have sat patiently and compassionately with the
truth of your sorrow and the hollowness of your grief. Taking the torch of
illumination and bravely shining its light into the darkest corners of your being,
you have recovered and are recovering the long-neglected and rejected parts
of yourself.

Through this process you have also become and are becoming the most
compassionate and kind parent your inner child could ever wish for and the
most noble and courageous companion your adult self could ever imagine.

Let's just let that sink in. Close your eyes, pause and take a deep heart-
embodied breath. Let's just arrive here in this moment together...

By valiantly facing your fear and pain, you have allowed your energetic blocks to be alchemized by the sweet medicine of gentleness, kindness and love. Tending compassionately to your trauma, you are integrating and releasing these memories from your physical, emotional and spiritual energy bodies.

You are the alchemist and healer of your family line. The seven generations that came before you and those that are yet to come thank you for your devotion and dedication.

Cross your arms at your chest and bring each hand to the opposite shoulder. Breathe here for a few moments. Give your shoulders a gentle squeeze and feel the power of your own embrace.

As you breathe, remember that you are so brave and have come so far. Know that now your mystic heart is your anchor, holding you steady on the seas of life. You are never alone; your family in the light are right by your side, and every day as you build your daily heart practice, you will feel them more and more.

Know that our time here is not a competition; you're not late or lagging behind. You're right on time. And *this* is your time. Your time to return home.

These last chapters are an invitation to return home to yourself in the deepest of ways. You're now able to listen to the wisdom of your heart and follow its lead. This is the beginning of your heart-embodied life. The time you've spent in your emotional heart has dissolved and shifted the barriers and limitations that had previously stood in the way of manifesting your greatest dreams and embodying your true potential.

Magic is inside you, and when your emotional heart is no longer blocked, that magic can finally flow through you.

There is magic inside you, and when your emotional heart is no longer blocked, that magic can finally flow through you. Being in your mystic heart with a sense of trust, belief and grace means you can uncover new facets of your being, and everything becomes possible...

This is where you'll unlock your cosmic blueprint and open to the beauty of the divine spark that lies at the core of your being, your True Essence...

Your True Essence

Create sacred space with a candle, incense, sage or resin. Bring your journal and make yourself really comfortable.

Light your candle in honour of how far you've come and the Light within you that is guiding you back to yourself...

Close your eyes and take four deep heart-embodied inhalations. Hold each one for five counts and release slowly. Feel the bones of your upper body soften and relax.

Visualize a path that takes you to a gate or a wooden door. This is the threshold to the mystic heart. Notice that you are barefoot and how your body is feeling in this moment. Turn the handle and step into your garden.

It's a beautiful bright morning. Feel the sun gently warming your face and the back of your neck. There are birds here, and bees, butterflies and dragonflies dancing on the breeze. Notice the soft green grass underfoot and the colours of the many different flowers in your garden. Stop for a moment and absorb the vibrant blues, purples, pinks, yellows, oranges and reds. You are surrounded by a sea of colour.

The beauty of Mother Nature is fully intact in this place. Everything is just as it should be. It's all in balance.

Breathe deeply and feel your shoulders drop completely as your core fully relaxes. You are safe.

You are walking into your garden. Each step you take adds to a deep cellular sense of freedom. Each step is a step of liberation.

You are here to find your golden seed, the seed that you planted at the very beginning of this process.

Has your seed grown into a tree, or is it a flower? Is this flower a rose? Trust the image that drops in for you.

If you have found a tree, sit underneath it and lean into the strength of its trunk. If your golden seed has blossomed into a flower, inhale its otherworldy perfume.

Place both hands on your heart and breathe. Breathe in the feelings of peace, stillness, grace, contentment, warmth, safety, wholeness and love that surround you and are you. This is your True Essence.

Breathe these feelings into your heart. Imagine they are pouring into your heart space and infusing it with golden light. Visualize this golden light flowing through the rest of your body.

From a corner of the garden, one of your guides is walking towards you. This is someone from your family in the light. Trust who comes in for you. It might be an angelic being, a family member, an ancestor or an animal. They are so happy to meet you here and so proud of you.

You are handed a pouch that contains four special seeds to plant in your garden. These are the seeds of expansion, imagination, creativity and aligned action. They will nourish, nurture and sustain the beauty of your inner gold, your True Essence.

Thank your guide and familiarize yourself with some of their features before you open your eyes. This will help you build a relationship with them in the future.

You can return to the garden and your golden seed whenever you need to be reminded of your True Essence.

Sowing the Seeds

Let's return to the power of intention for a moment and get clear on why you're sowing the seeds of expansion, imagination, creativity and aligned action.

Know that they will support the expression of your True Essence. You're choosing to live an authentic life, the life that you truly deserve to be living and breathing in this moment. You are here because you are looking to discover, express and live out your purpose, the reason your soul chose to be here. These seeds will nourish this awakening...

'May our heart's garden of awakening bloom with hundreds of flowers.'
THICH NHAT HANH

Expansion

The opposite of expansion is contraction and constriction, and most of us are stuck in this state without even realizing it. We're conditioned to deny who we are or who we might become. We're afraid to take risks or that first crucial step because we think we'll be rejected, humiliated or fail.

But our souls are naturally expansive because our true nature originates from oceans of infinite divine consciousness. It's incarnation that conditions us into forgetfulness, into cosmic amnesia...

When we were children, before our stories unfolded, we were so much more in touch with our natural magic.

Before we became cynical, jaded and disconnected, either through disappointment, rejection and neglect or by being sent to schools where we were taught not to feel, we naturally spent more time in our magical mystic heart. We were playful and our sweetness and innocence helped us view the world with wonder and awe. We believed in all sorts of stuff from Father Christmas to the tooth fairy. We were curious, open and expansive. Not only did we have a wonderfully wild and vivid imagination, but we were also generally more connected to nature and attuned to inter-dimensional space, the world beyond the veil of this dimension.

Many of my clients will suddenly remember how they were able to see or feel auras, angels, elementals in nature or family members who had passed over in their childhood. Fear shut that second sight down.

Don't worry if you don't resonate with the imaginative, curious child I'm describing here; you can still experience the magic of this energy today – you'll simply be activating it within you for the first time.

•••

Before we continue, I'd like to introduce you to the bundle of magic that my younger self embodied and that led to this moment where I find myself writing these words for you, right here, right now, some 45 years later...

My mother had an old leather-bound journal that I was completely mesmerized by. It had soft, well-worn pages and somehow smelled of a life she had lived before I was born. There were handpicked recipes there, stuffed in among her lists of things to do and occasional observations about life.

These words were written on the inside cover:

'What the mind can conceive and believe, it can achieve.
It is essential to evaluate positive thoughts against negative ones.'
NAPOLEON HILL

I didn't consciously understand what these words meant, but a part of me knew that they equated to something very special, and as I read and reread them, they were seeded into my unconscious mind.

When I was older, I learned that Napoleon Hill, born in 1883, was one of the first ever self-help authors, writing the first modern book about manifestation, *Think and Grow Rich*, which has sold over 100 million copies worldwide.

Fast-forward to sometime around 1995. I'm 23 and I've just returned from another back-packing adventure in a far-flung place like Central America or India. I'm inspired by my mother's extraordinary tales of her own intrepid trips and treks in the sixties, but there's also a significant part of me that's running away from the uncertainty of an unknown future.

I'm broke and move back home with my mum, which at this time still brings its own set of challenges. Added to that, most of my friends have settled into jobs and careers. To me, they all feel very grown-up. A strange sense of running out of time begins to confront me, an ominous rising fear that I've been left behind.

We can all experience this 'running out of time' feeling at any age, for a myriad of different reasons and I hear these words often from my clients. If you're feeling this now, know that we always have time. *You're right on time!* For all of it.

So, take a moment to think about what more love, abundance or success looks like to you. Will you be attracting a new romance or a different type of partner or relationship? You might want to find or change careers or work less. Do you fantasize about picking up a new interest or starting a new business or creative project? Perhaps you long to develop some healthy habits as a gesture of self-love, or travel, settle down or start a family. Whatever you secretly wish for, when you plant the seed of expansion, you remove the blinkers and give yourself the gift of mystic vision. You get to connect to the quantum field, where everything is possible...

Back in 1995, whilst anxiety has started to creep into my awareness, I'm not completely overwhelmed by it. Meditating from an early age has helped me understand that we are so much more than our thoughts and the ego mind that creates those thoughts. So, I do exactly what Napoleon suggested: I take a moment and right-size my negative, fear-based thoughts. I notice them, then choose not to spend time with them. I redirect my energy and continue showing up for my dream.

I remember my inner voice guided me to write down my desires and wishes for my future on a single sheet of A4 paper. The guidance was very clear:

'Give yourself permission to dream the greatest of dreams, Estelle. You have unlimited potential. And in the field of possibility there are no edges, there are no ceilings and there are no stop signs. Everything is possible here. And because time is an illusion, you can start today.'

The field of possibility is the quantum field or pure consciousness, and when we're accessing this reality, our ability to manifest our greatest dreams finally becomes possible in real time.

As I said earlier, we're never running out of time. The universe just needs us to trust, expand and actually show up at the ballpark to be part of this game of life.

A heart-embodied life waters our seed of expansion and picks our front-row seats at the same time! When we lean in to the slipstream of expansion energy, our outcomes change. From the moment we wake up and open our eyes, every fibre of our being is automatically engaged with the adventure of life. Every cell is curious and open to what could happen next and what might be around the corner for us. We begin to witness, through signs and synchronicities, that the universe hasn't forgotten us or left us behind.

When we expand into the world, we are co-creators of the cosmic dance. We become master manifesters and experience deeply embodied joy, connection and creativity.

Drop into your heart space now and connect with your inner child.

Reflect on what they believed in and what they could see or feel in the world.

Ask yourself how you can expand more and become more adventurous in your life. Finish this sentence: 'I've always wanted to try…'

Choose one thing that will push you out of your comfort zone and expand your world in this moment. It might help to consider something you have been putting off or procrastinating over. Is it time to start dating or editing your employment details to send out into the world, or to contact a family member or friend? You may commit to adding a new walk to your weekly routine or choose to smile more at strangers in the street. There's no right or wrong here. For Annisa, it was dancing...

My healing journey with Estelle brought me to a point where I needed to cut loose from my normal isolating routine and expand more into my life.

We spoke about how movement could help me. Previously, I'd felt shy and awkward when dancing in the presence of others, but I decided to take a leap of faith and it's been utterly life-changing for me. I feel connected to my joy, creativity and sensuality for the first time ever. I've discovered the spontaneous creativity that arises from focusing within, moving my body in weird and wonderful ways that reflect my individuality.

By resting my busy mind and tuning in to the power of music, I've also unearthed my sensuality. My feminine essence has naturally arisen and flows through me.

I now know what it means to 'feel alive', to be in the fullness that the present moment has to offer, and I am learning to reflect this off the dance floor in my day-to-day life too.

Annisa

Annisa found powerful healing and transformation in trying something she hadn't enjoyed before. It's our birthright to dance, sing and play as we need to. These are some of the ways our souls express themselves creatively in the world.

The reclaiming of these parts of ourselves forms an integral part of the manifestation of our True Essence.

Imagination and Creativity

'Imagination is more important than knowledge. For knowledge is limited to all we now know and understand, while imagination embraces the entire world, and all there ever will be to know and understand.'

ALBERT EINSTEIN

Sowing the seeds of imagination and creativity in your garden will rewrite your life's script and change its trajectory. Imagination is the true inspiration behind all great leaders, writers, musicians, scientists, entrepreneurs, architects and artists. It's a formidable superpower. The life that you are living right now is an expression of how much you have allowed your unique and powerful imagination to joyfully and limitlessly 'embrace the entire world'... or not.

'The man who has no imagination has no wings.'

MUHAMMED ALI

Imagination and creativity are also the ways that the Divine moves through us. Creativity actions imagination and helps us bring our new ideas and downloads into form. When our heart expands into the sacred flow of this holy slipstream, we impact the frequency of our families, communities and the world in profound ways.

In 1916, Albert Einstein presented this field equation to the Prussian Academy of Sciences in Berlin:

$$G=8nT$$

Healing is making the choice to only

surround yourself with frequencies

that support your soul's growth.

At a time when technology was a good 90 years away from developing a telescope that could penetrate into deepest space, Einstein had discovered evidence for the existence of a previously unimagined cosmic body – the black hole.

What's most striking about this discovery is that it didn't originate from the external world. Sitting with only pen and paper, Einstein allowed his mind to roam beyond the boundaries of accepted reality. His *imagination* was allowed to imagine. And it had a field day!

Nothing exists in this dimension until it has first been imagined. No one ventured to the moon until someone looked into space and imagined themselves up there. No one built computers, performed open-heart surgery, survived beyond 45, lived in brick houses or even used fire until someone thought, *I wonder what would happen if...*

> *'What is now proved was once only imagined.'*
> **WILLIAM BLAKE**

Remember all of our imaginative efforts, be they known or unknown, are of great consequence, because we're all connected, so each contribution affects the whole. The moment our imagination flies unfettered into a limitless sky, we begin to live our purpose. And this creates harmony within the entire macrocosm.

It's not always easy to expand into this flow, though. Prolific 20th-century painter and sculptor Pablo Picasso famously declared, 'Every child is an artist. The problem is how to remain an artist when we grow up.' Today this couldn't resonate more. Our precious daydreaming time has been eroded or lost altogether as we've been bombarded by phones, screens and social media.

You might also find that your imagination and creativity have been hijacked by external and internal judgement, cynicism and perfectionism.

Know that a repressed imagination leads to malaise of the spirit.

> '*The best use of imagination is creativity.*
> *The worst use of imagination is anxiety.*'
> DEEPAK CHOPRA

So, nurture openness, curiosity and trust and let those creative juices flow.

Activating and nourishing the creative aspects of your being might be about painting or writing more, or exploring dancing, arts, crafts or music. Gift yourself the space to rediscover something about yourself or try something new.

I loved art as a child. Once I got to high school and into my teenage years, though, I didn't feel good enough to even try, so I focused on more analytical achievements that would help me tick boxes.

Fast-forward to age 25, when I was working with my energy centres, especially my root chakra, on my healing journey with Estelle and I turned to art as a way to express a breakthrough that I couldn't articulate in words. I began painting different parts of my healing journey, including moments of grief and the angels I felt protected by.

I now use art as a meditation and imagine each stroke releasing emotion I want to let go of. I have found my recent paintings really move people in a way they may not have felt had I used words. Art truly soothes my soul.

Spending time in my creative energy is also a gift for my inner child. It reminds me that life is meant to be lived slow, in a state of flow, and that mistakes will happen on the canvas. Life to me is one big messy painting, full of expression and authenticity.

Abby

How can we stimulate our creativity? Deadlines and task-focused thoughts may do it, but the magic really happens when we expose ourselves to new experiences and give our brain time to conceptualize new things. Not really thinking at all is even better. Research suggests that when we daydream or allow our mind to wander, with no fixed agenda or particular place to go, we are generally more intelligent!

The seeds of imagination and creativity can also help you find answers to the smaller issues that arise every day – how to parent or relate to partners, friends or work colleagues more harmoniously, how to negotiate time and resources more effectively or how to find solutions to projects or situations when you can't see a way through. These seeds are transformational in many ways and will begin the bigger process of unlocking your true purpose.

> *'I saw the angel in the marble, and carved until I set it free.'*
> MICHELANGELO

You are the angel and you are also the artist. Get to work and set yourself free...

Aligned Action

> *'It is the combination of thought and love which forms
> the irresistible force of the law of attraction.'*
> CHARLES HAMMEL

What is aligned action and why is it so important to plant this seed in the garden? Aligned action is about being clear about your hopes and dreams, then showing up and taking the appropriate steps towards them every day. Having discovered our True Essence, we can now manifest it with aligned action. The potential for manifestation exists within every one of us. And once you've activated this potential, you will take that ability with you into the rest of your incarnation.

For now, let's return to my first-ever vision board. I began to draw my dreams in a super-naïve and simplistic way on a blank page, but my intention was really solid. I drew a stick person in the middle of the blank white sheet and wrote 'Estelle' above her head. Then I drew lines from the stick person to things I wanted to manifest. The main one was becoming a television presenter. At that time, I didn't have a hope in hell of getting into TV. In fact, I didn't even have a job. But I still put it out there.

Within months, I had landed a job as a personal assistant to two commissioning executives at the BBC. I can't say I was the most efficient of assistants, but I was grateful to be in the building of my dreams and a step closer to fulfilling them.

It wasn't easy. My faith would wane and my morale would sink to all-time lows. But every day as I walked the hour to and from work, I would use that time to keep my dream alive. I would literally think positive thoughts about my dream and imagine that it had already happened. This built an unshakable sense of conviction and belief inside me.

Heart-based positive thoughts and affirmations erode dense matter. Slowly but surely, they have the power to create grooves where before there was solid mass. Be the river that creates a way through where there wasn't one before. Even the smallest specks of sand are carving new ways of being as the river flows constantly onward. Before you know it, there is a way through, a glimmer of light, a glimmer of hope, created by positive thoughts – not toxic by-passy positive thoughts, but ones grounded in a growing sense of your authentic self.

> *'As a single footstep will not make a path on the earth, so a*
> *single thought will not make a pathway in the mind.*
> *To make a deep physical path, we walk again and again.*
> *To make a deep mental path, we must think over and over*
> *the kind of thoughts we wish to dominate in our lives.'*
> **Henry David Thoreau**

An invaluable nugget of wisdom I learned from the time that I spent at the BBC manifesting my dream is that *no one knows you as well as you know yourself*, so if *you* can conceive it, then it's up to *you* to achieve it.

Don't keep those thoughts to yourself – tell the world about them.

At five o'clock on the dot we would all squeeze into the steel-grey lift and often we would end up discussing our future plans.

'A TV presenter,' I would say every time. 'I'm a TV presenter.'

I would always state that fact in the present tense, affirming that reality every day as if it had already happened.

Speaking the dream out is loud is a huge leap of faith. It takes guts. If you are surrounded by judgemental, jealous or resentful people who are basically motivated by fear rather than love *and* if you care about what they think of you, feelings of shame or embarrassment will naturally emerge from boldly speaking your truth. These people may look to ridicule you and their opinions may make you feel a bit wobbly or undermined. The unspoken messaging can be that you're getting ideas above your station – who do you think you are?

Remember these people might be convincing, but they are battling their own worthlessness, self-hatred and inner demons. The great news is that much of the work we have done together is helping you release the need for external validation.

Of course, no one else could imagine me working in children's television or hosting a hip-hop music show on the BBC World Service or interviewing Destiny's Child for BBC Radio 2 or writing music articles for glossy magazines or working on three travel shows at the same time, because *my* purpose was unique to *me* and the energy of all of those possibilities was buried inside me alone. You will be the only person who gets a true sense of *your* purpose at a cellular level. So, it's time to get behind your own vision and be your greatest cheerleader. Trust the calling and the adventure that is yours and yours alone.

Interestingly, my boyfriend at the time was super-negative about life. He was forever reeling off *negative* 'facts' about *my* dream. Things like: 'But everyone wants to be a television presenter, don't they?' and 'Why would you want to do that? It's *so* competitive' and 'You've never done anything like that before, why on Earth would they choose you?' and 'You're way too old to be on TV.'

This was Negative Boyfriend's truth. And because he believed everything he said, he would have created that reality for himself if it had been his personal dream to be a television presenter, and also for me if I had spent any time buying into his negativity.

I had chosen a partner who was recreating the negative, critical programming that I had experienced growing up in my family home. Initially, we need to learn how to separate ourselves from what we have known and from our own negative thoughts. Separation from the inner or outer critic can be a big challenge when we are literally co-creating a reality that is new and unfamiliar to us.

It was true that I had no idea what it really meant to work in front of the camera. I hadn't grown up around anyone who had worked in the media, there were few women of colour on screen at that time and there was nothing in my life so far to suggest that I would be particularly good at presenting. But there I was at 23, having *decided* in no uncertain terms that I was a television presenter. Period.

A year later I was presenting my first show on BBC1. And it was no great surprise that the boyfriend was no longer on the scene to witness that moment.

Lose the Negative Vibes

Be mindful of the negative voices that surround you as you watch your seeds grow. Words shape reality. Notice how you feel after being with different people. It might be time to leave some of them to their own devices and negative vibes. If that's not possible, just noticing how you are being negatively impacted is very empowering in itself and will invite you to use your voice to set some much-needed boundaries.

Healing is making the choice to only surround yourself with frequencies that support your soul's growth.

A huge part of the healing journey is evaluating who is enriching your energy and who is draining it. When we stay in relationships that drain our spirits, we are energetically sabotaging ourselves. Ask yourself these questions:

- Can these friends/family members only relate to the old version of me or can they support my growth?

- Does their energy throw me off-balance?

- Am I over-stimulated and stressed in their company?

- Do I struggle to show up authentically with them?

- Does the relationship seem forced and habitual?

- Do I feel that they have taken away any good energy I had?

- Do they use humour or passive-aggressive communication to shame and undermine me?

- Do they diminish my problems and play up their own?

- Do they display self-centred or egocentric behaviour?

- Are they surrounded by a constant cycle of chaos and drama and do they often draw me into it?

- Do they allow me to feel seen or heard?

- Do they think the world revolves around them?

Valuing your time and energy is actually a radical act of self-love. Protecting the vibration of your embryonic dreams from being trampled by naysayers is also crucial to ensuring that your precious golden seed sees the light of day.

naysayer
noun • often disapproving
someone who says something is not possible, is not good, or will fail:
• *He ignored the naysayers and persevered.*
CAMBRIDGE ENGLISH DICTIONARY

A good question to reflect upon right now is what part of this archetype do you recognize in yourself? Is there a little bit of your Shadow still lurking? If you relate to any of the naysayer traits, now is the perfect time to start taking some compassionate accountability for this aspect of yourself.

To break the naysayer habit:

- Begin to notice when the impulse arises within you to undermine someone else's light or positivity.

- Take a breath and don't say a word.

- Journal about the incident and use your heart-embodied ancestors meditation (*see page 191*) to question the origins of your resentment.

Words do hold power. Choose to keep your personal power intact and your energy vibrating at a high frequency by removing yourself from gossip or being a Debbie Downer and raining on someone else's parade. Stay in your own lane and get your own parade illuminated and fabulous! It's waiting for you!

The takeaways from this story are:

- Anchoring into our mystic heart neutralizes and right-sizes negative thoughts and helps us to dare to dream without limitations.

- The restoration of our sense of expansion and curiosity, imagination and creativity can happen when we spend more time connected to this space.

- Words have power. Don't let the words of others steer you away from your destination. Surround yourself with people whose energy mirrors your own.

- If necessary, alchemize the naysayer archetype within.

Your Cosmic Canvas

What now? Well, I suggest it's time to have some fun manifesting the life you were born for. Why not paint the picture of your future onto your very own cosmic canvas?

You can actually buy a canvas from an art shop, but if that's not possible, get creative with a piece of paper. Gather magazines, print images and buy some acrylic paint and artist's supplies if you want to. Remind yourself that there is no right or wrong here. This is your magic and your adventure.

Light a candle, invoke angels and your family in the light, and honour the slipstream of expansion and infinite possibility.

Lie down and place your hands on your heart chakra.

Focus on breathing in expansiveness. Imagine your heart space softening and expanding with each inhalation.

Imagine your heart as light. With each exhalation, this light expands into the room. Fill the room with the energy of your heart and then push it out beyond the windows, the ceiling and the roof of your home.

Visualize yourself in a scenario where one of your dreams has come true and you are experiencing all of the feelings you would feel. Give permission for the sensations of relief, excitement, pride, happiness and joy to wash over you.

Take yourself through the same process with another of your dreams.

This is something to add to your daily practice. Just spend a few moments each day walking yourself through a scenario in which you have already reached one of your goals. You can do this making tea, walking the dog or waiting for the bus. Let your mind drift and really enjoy bringing your dreams into this dimension.

Print images from the internet or cut them out from magazines or get out your artist's materials and illustrate that scenario of success.

Think about how you would describe what happened and how you felt; for example, 'I imagined finding a new partner and a sensation of feeling safe and loved washed over me.' Add those words to your canvas.

'Everything you can imagine is real.'
PABLO PICASSO

'Cherish your visions and your dreams, as they are the children of your soul, the blueprint of your ultimate achievements.'
NAPOLEON HILL

The entire world is your cosmic canvas – a blank canvas with no edges that is yours alone to fill, imagine and re-imagine every day, a place of hidden mysteries that are yearning for you to know them, of dreams that are longing for you to dream them...

CHAPTER 10

Homecoming

'I have reached the inner vision and through Thy spirit in me,
I have heard Thy wondrous secret.
Through Thy mystic insight,
Thou hast caused a spring
of knowledge to well up within me,
a fountain of power, pouring forth living waters,
a flood of love and of all-embracing wisdom
like the splendour of eternal Light.'
'THE BOOK OF HYMNS', THE DEAD SEA SCROLLS

There are absolutely no coincidences in life, and when you chose to read this book at this particular moment in your incarnation, you were responding to a deep yearning. This yearning may have been completely unconscious, but your heart was calling you home, and you listened. And as our time together is coming to an end in this form, know that this pilgrimage to the chambers of the heart has gifted you with sacred knowledge. Entering your mystic heart and inhabiting this final chamber has taught you something about your innate wholeness and soul wisdom that you will carry with you forever.

As you now know, your mystic heart is a place of great beauty, a cathedral of infinite light spiralling within you, the home of your True Essence, your soul. Your soul is a divine flame of stillness. A spark of light that is eternal and can never be extinguished. It's your inner gold.

The reunification of your Earth self with your True Essence is your life's greatest love story.

When we return to the wisdom of our soul energy and the arms of the Divine, we remember the fabric of our original nature. We are woven from love. There is nothing more precious here than that, nothing more cherished in this moment than you.

You've been expanding your felt-sense knowing of love by showing up for yourself in new ways through the different initiations you have experienced. Each stage of this process of transmuting the energy of your trauma, patterns, emotions and story into unique and beautiful wisdom has been a radical practice of self-love, walking you home...

In this process, you have taken the reins of your life back from your ego. Now it becomes possible for you to surrender to the idea that love is at your core. By default, love is beauty. Unlocking this truth gives you a chance to peek at the glow of your inner beauty. To finally accept yourself and love everything that you see reflected back at you in the mirror.

There's a treasure trove within you.

Imagine golden light pouring through your crown, flooding your heart space. Then repeat this affirmation out loud:

'I am love.

*I have arrived from love, and when this
life is done, I will return to love.*

*I give myself permission in this moment
to embrace my True Essence.*

*I give myself permission to acknowledge
that my True Essence is love.*

I honour the undeniable power of love and beauty.

*I give myself permission to live that beauty, to express
that beauty and to embody that beauty.*

I am a channel for love and I am a channel for beauty.

I am creating beauty in the world every day.

Just by being alive. Just by being myself.

And so it is. And so it is. And so it is.

Blessed Be/Amen/Ase.'

Close your eyes for a few moments and if the energy feels stuck in any way or if you need to give permission for the words to land in your psyche again, repeat them once or twice more.

Return to this affirmation by adding it to your practice.

So, what changes when we honour our inner beauty and lead a more soulful existence? What do we manifest when more of our choices emanate from a frequency of love rather than fear? What happens when we meet life from a heart-embodied place?

When we anchor into our mystic heart, we've found our North Star and safe harbour. We can finally hear and listen to our own intuition and have the power to manifest more love, purpose and connection in our life...

In a way it still feels odd to acknowledge this, but life just feels real in its totality. It doesn't feel performative any more, as there's no more need for hiding or pretending that those Shadow parts don't exist. All those parts that were hiding in my Shadow can finally breathe and see the light of day.

And when those parts that were suppressed are seen, show up through a connection or just by truly living life, it becomes a tender acknowledgement and an opportunity to give those parts of myself the love they always needed.

Since these changes of self-love and self-acceptance, the direction of my life has become more consistent, easy and flowing. I am showing up for my purpose more and have a growing eagerness to follow through on my goals. One of them is pursuing my artistic career as a photographer. The inherent hurdles of pursuing that dream don't overwhelm me any more.

Instead, they just feel like part of the adventure, the needed growing edges to manifest and actualize my dream career.

Will

When we anchor into our mystic heart, we can finally hear and listen to our own intuition and have the power to manifest more love, purpose and connection in our life.

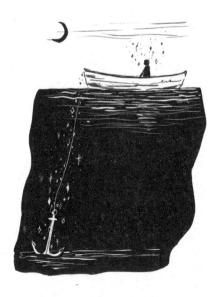

A heart-embodied life wakes up our inner fire and passion. We find and begin to use our authentic voice, harnessing the courage to speak up where before we were afraid to. Communicating our needs and our boundaries from a place of inner calm is a game-changer. This means we can hold ourselves safe and we're no longer terrified of being seen by others.

It's safe to be all aspects of who we are – vulnerable, empowered, compassionate and unapologetically unrestrained and carefree. This is what joy feels like. And freedom...

> When I think back to the person I was four years ago, I almost don't recognize myself. I've shed that version of myself, healing internally so that the true 'me' is now able to step to the forefront of my life.
>
> I had many different aspects of myself to alchemize: past trauma, Shadow sides, projections, co-dependency, complete lack of self-love and awareness. But today I no longer question who I am, what I think, what I want from life or where I'm going. My True Essence has become so strong that in a way she leads and I'm there to take whatever action is needed to manifest my reality. People talk about being the 'best version of yourself', but now there is no 'version', it's just me, as the True Essence of who I have always been, and it is so great to finally know and be her.
>
> Elisha

We're constantly evolving, learning and processing different layers of experience, of course, so there'll always be growing pains. We'll still be presented with challenges, too; sometimes life just doesn't go to plan and really hurts. I can't guarantee that you won't be hit by the occasional curveball.

Life absolutely *loves* a curveball! Life is life and it does what it does. It's messy because it's supposed to be!

But the big difference is that from this moment onwards you will be guided more and more by your True Essence. This means that you're finally in the driving seat of your own lifetime. Less second-guessing, dysregulation, confusion, disconnection, overwhelm and anxiety. Through this process you have taken the power back, and it's well and truly your time to be seen, to be heard and to shine.

It's been three years since my legs turned to jelly on the white stairs of Estelle's flat. I've since met various versions of myself on her sofa under a multitude of multi-coloured crystals – I feel as if I've shed a thousand skins. In all honesty, I barely recognize the person I once was.

A few months after my first Estelle session, my then closed-off and broken heart began to open. I've since gone on to experience the profound power and true meaning of intimacy. And not just romantically, but in every interaction, whether that's with friends, in my work, or with family.

This makes it sound as if my life suddenly transformed into unicorns and rainbows – far from it. If someone were to ask me, 'Why bother doing the work?' my answer would be clear: 'It's the only way to weather the storm.'

It is in times of trouble that we come to truly see what we are made of. Six months ago, my mother was diagnosed with cancer. Various other traumatic events have made it feel like my world is crumbling around me, and yet the ground beneath is now rock solid. I'm not sure my health or my heart would have been capable of withstanding these events before. Doing the work has given me a core of steel. I am now both soft and boundaried. I know when to take action and how to hold myself safe.

I'd love to rejoice, kick back and shout, 'Look, Estelle! We did it! I am healed! I have manifested everything! Life is a breeze!' but that's not quite how life works. And that's okay because I am here, I am alive and I have an unshakeable strength because I chose to do the work.

Kit

Now you are anchored in your mystic heart, you, too, can find strength when you need to, and you may encounter everyday miracles as well:

I was recently divorced, having been married for 12 years. I was living life thinking everything was okay, but it really wasn't okay. I was completely lost and felt numb inside. I was like a swan on the surface, but underneath I didn't feel connected or grounded in any way.

I wanted to connect with my authentic self, break free and be that butterfly who finds her wings. We protect ourselves with all of these walls and what I've learned from this process is that our safe space comes from knocking those walls down. Your roots are within you.

Four months ago, after starting my heart work, I found myself at my mother's bedside, guiding her into the next life. My relationship with my mother had been deeply fractured and distant my whole life and in recent years she had also suffered from dementia, so there was an added layer of hurt and trauma from the lies she would tell about me.

Before I started working with Estelle I could go into a church or a wood and could feel a different energy, but could never create a space like that for myself. But in the hospital, I was able to drop into my heart and nothing that came before mattered any more. I made peace. I can't quite put into words the power of the healing that came from that experience. It was such an extraordinary gift and a privilege. I was in a state of grace the whole time as my mother transitioned. The way I was able to be of service to love and the family line was a miracle for me...

Emma

Your Purpose

Now you have crossed the threshold to your mystic heart, you are able to access your cosmic blueprint, which will support you in manifesting your purpose. That is why your soul chose to be here.

Your cosmic blueprint is the treasure within you. It contains your unique codes of co-creation and manifestation. Activating this cosmic blueprint reconnects you with your most cherished dreams and desires and helps you imagine limitless new ones. Then you can manifest the life you were born for, live your purpose and embody the love that is your original nature. You will take your rightful place and space in the world, bright lights illuminating the beauty and majesty of your magnificent being for all to see, hear and feel your brilliance. The world needs you to be alive and awake to all that you are. Now more than ever before...

What is your purpose here? Will you risk accomplishing it? Will you show up for it or will you turn your back on it and return to what you already know?'

Before we go on, let me make one thing very clear, in no uncertain terms: *everyone has a path that they alone must travel.* Along that path, they will encounter their purpose. No one – I repeat, *no one* – gets down here without a path or a purpose. Including you. You wouldn't be on the planet otherwise. Period.

We often have more than one purpose in this lifetime, and sometimes our purpose may be to rest and do nothing, but we have a divine purpose too. So, there is our 'what we came to the planet to achieve' type of purpose and our 'daily' purpose, which might feel mundane in the light of what we would like to achieve in our entire lifetime, but is an invaluable and intrinsic part of the journey.

Today our purpose might just be to walk instead of taking the bus. Or to drink a herbal tea instead of a teeth-chattering double espresso. It might be to not drink alcohol or to resist reacting when hit by a wave of anger.

The purpose of this moment might be to spend time with our children or love a friend more. You've been learning how to speak more kindly to yourself during those in-between times that only you really know about, instead of shrinking at the sound of the inner critic. These small things are profound in themselves. Never lose sight of this truth.

But back to the bigger purpose now. Think of yours as a unique golden ticket that God stuffs in your back pocket just as you head off to Earth for another incarnation. And this is by no means just any old purpose either. It's the one that your higher self agreed to and the reason why it decided to sign up for the emotional cacophony of life again – the ups, the downs, the ebb, the flow, the joy, pain, tears, laughter, hopelessness, helplessness. The general hope is that at some point you'll remember that the ticket is there.

If you can just contemplate for a moment or two the possibility of a divine plan, then you won't risk missing the ride of your life!

Yet destiny and co-creation can actually present us with a truly perplexing paradox. If we are born with a specific *purpose*, a chosen *destiny*, a pre-ordained *fate*, how can we possibly miss the boat? It's written in the stars, isn't it? Surely destiny is destiny? Whatever we're doing, wherever we find ourselves, we'll just happen upon it. It'll fall out of the sky and land slap bang in front of us, like a meteorite or some other piece of cosmic debris, right? *Wrong!*

Let's just clear this up right now. The idea that destiny will go out of its way to personally hunt *us* down, find *our* post code and break *our* door down is a widely held misconception.

The fundamental truth is: we have to show up in the first place!

Showing up can just mean that we've changed our headspace. Tuned the antennae to the frequencies of ideas and creativity.

Do this and you'll find your purpose waiting for you like a long-lost friend, deeply relieved that you aren't actually as flaky as you've been threatening to be or, worse still, running for the hills. You're manifesting your True Essence.

> *'You cannot travel the path*
> *until you have become the path itself.'*
> BUDDHA

Your purpose doesn't belong to anyone else but *you*. So, it's up to *you* to get this show on the road. Engage the ignition and put your foot on the pedal. Otherwise, we'll be hanging out in this bland-looking cul-de-sac for quite some time. Could be a lifetime!

When clients come to see me who are struggling with their purpose, I am often given the visual of a very dense wood – so dense that a giant canopy of leaves shuts out much of the sunlight. It resembles the Black Forest in Germany or perhaps somewhere in the Canadian Rockies. Think medieval Black Forest... pre-logging.

So here we are, my client and me, wandering around in ever-decreasing circles in this incredibly dense, dark wood. Lost. Unsurprisingly, said client is looking for a way out of the murk. Desperate for a map, a compass, a torch, a smartphone app perhaps, they'll take anything that they can get their hands on.

'How the hell do I get out of here?' they ask me, looking ruefully down at their feet, afraid they'll just be trudging round the same circle and the same bunch of medieval firs. Again.

'Just get on the path!' I reply.

They look up for a second, quizzically. 'There isn't a path!' comes the indignant retort. 'Can't you see I'm stuck in a really weird place? You know I can't see the wood for the trees! If I could, I'd have rolled out of here ages ago.'

Well at this point, I'll definitely tip my hat to their powerful self-hypnosis techniques. It appears that they truly believe that they are a prisoner. They're utterly convinced that they have been condemned to exist in the shadows of their greatness. On the peripheries, in this bizarre twilight zone. Forever.

Are you that client?

Close your eyes, place your hands on your heart.

Take your time to feel fully attuned to your mystical heart and then ask it these questions:

~   What is my lifetime purpose?

~   What is my daily purpose?

~ What are the steps I can take to meet my life purpose?

~ What are the steps I can take to meet my daily purpose?

Now you know what to do.

Manifesting our True Essence activates our cosmic blueprint and connects us to our purpose, too.

And we all have our stories, until we don't... until we are liberated from the shackles of our stories. When we alchemize our stories, we create space for new ones to emerge.

For years, my heart was sealed shut by layers of self-protection. But at the retreat, a group of men who were strangers, men who I would never have met in my everyday life, became part of my healing. Their support helped me redefine the essence of masculinity and, more crucially, to see myself as a man who was strong, loving and worthy of love.

After my breakthrough I started a relationship with someone who accepted me for who I was, and together we navigated the complexities of a real relationship. Instead of retreating at the first signs of trouble, as I would have before, we tackled challenges together, which only deepened our bond. I learned that to love and be loved isn't just about joy, it's also about growing stronger through the trials. This understanding was just the beginning of a deeply transformative year.

I also changed my relationship with food, which I'd used as a shield against feelings of unworthiness. Gone were the days of emotional eating and yo-yo dieting. I committed to personal training, challenging old labels from my youth of 'He's not the sporty one.'

The result was a 40-kilo weight loss in less than 12 months, a physical manifestation of my internal transformation.

My entrepreneurial spirit found its outlet, too. The children's brand I had long dreamed of creating came to life. I worked through the twists, turns and bumps, launching products that now delight children and support parents across the USA. Their glowing feedback is a testament to the brand's impact: 'So in love with this cuddly comfort! A treasure in our home.' 'Beyond adorable! He stole our hearts.' 'Bringing calm to our nights and joy throughout the day.' And many more...

So, in a single year, three remarkable shifts occurred: love found me quickly, I reclaimed my health and I journeyed towards prosperity. The retreat marked a significant change of course, proving that our greatest strength comes from the bravery to be vulnerable and the willingness to redefine our path.

I'll be honest, the idea of attending a retreat made me nervous. It was a leap into the unknown, far outside the boundaries of my usual routine. Yet, something within me – a quiet but persistent determination – compelled me to go for it. That decision has reshaped my life, though not without its share of bumps along the way. This isn't fantasy; it's real life, with real challenges. But when you commit to delving deep and facing your vulnerabilities head on, the rewards are unparalleled. I share this experience to encourage others. We all have the inner strength to push beyond our perceived limits. If you're on the verge of a life-altering decision, embrace it. Your actions and courage are the keys to unlocking the life you're destined to live. It may not be easy, but it's worth it.

Jonathan

Manifesting our True Essence

activates our cosmic blueprint and

connects us to our purpose, too.

Be at One

When we arrive in the chamber of the mystical heart, we love ourselves enough to be at one with ourselves. It is here alone that we can fully understand how to be at one with all things, as all feelings of not belonging dissolve.

If the rock is made up of energy just like the tree, the ocean, beast, fish, fowl, man, woman, child, what really separates us? It is *form* alone. Your journey to this moment has brought you into relationship with this truth.

These realizations awaken true sight within us and then everything appears as it truly is. We break through this material dimension of form and are delivered quite literally into the light. We penetrate the veil of the seen world and perceive what lies within the unseen world.

> '*I was standing on the highest mountain of them all, and round*
> *about beneath me was the whole hoop of the world.*
> *And while I stood there, I saw more than I can tell and I*
> *understood more than I saw; for I was seeing in a sacred*
> *manner the shapes of all things in the spirit, and the shape*
> *of all shapes as they must live together like one being.*
> *And I say the sacred hoop of my people was one of the many hoops*
> *that made one circle, wide as daylight and as starlight, and in the*
> *center grew one mighty flowering tree to shelter all the children*
> *of one mother and one father. And I saw that it was holy...*
> *But anywhere is the center of the world.*'
>
> BLACK ELK

The hoop is a circle of connection. The connection that energy has to energy, regardless of form, is truly sacred. When human consciousness recognizes the interconnectedness of all things, it is at once profoundly humbling and empowering.

'Remember that wherever your heart is,
there you will find your treasure.'
PAULO COELHO

If you take anything away with you from this book, it should be your heart. Remember your heart every day. Check in with your heart wherever you are. Go through life gently, compassionately and with grace. Stay open and curious to the magic that surrounds you in the unseen world. Pay the love of your awakening forward. Love, and love some more...

Trust that you were born to be a channel for everyday miracles. You are a miracle.

Let your little bird soar, fly among the stars and sleep when she needs to in the cradle of your heart.

You've got this...

Recommended Reading

Coleman Barks, *A Year with Rumi: Daily Readings*, HarperCollins, 2006

John Bradshaw, *Healing the Shame That Binds You*, Health Communications, Inc., 2006

Paulo Coelho, *The Alchemist*, HarperCollins, 1995

Deborah A. Dana and Stephen W. Porges, *The Polyvagal Theory in Therapy: Engaging the Rhythm of Regulation*, W.W. Norton & Co., 2018

Norman Doidge, *The Brain That Changes Itself: Stories of Personal Triumph from the Frontiers of Brain Science*, Penguin, 2008

Louise Hay and friends, *Gratitude: A Way of Life*, Hay House, 1996

Napoleon Hill, *Think and Grow Rich*, Soho Books, 1937

Richard Hycner, *Between Person and Person: Toward a Dialogical Psychotherapy*, Gestalt Journal Press, 1991

Peter A. Levine, *Waking the Tiger: Healing Trauma*, North Atlantic Books, 1997

Pia Mellody, *Facing Codependence: What It Is, Where It Comes from, How It Sabotages Our Lives*, HarperOne, 2002

Pia Mellody, *Facing Love Addiction: Giving Yourself the Power to Change the Way You Love*, HarperOne, 2003

M. G. Mokgobi, 'Understanding traditional African healing', *African Journal for Physical Health Education, Recreation and Dance* 20 (September 2014) (Suppl. 2), 24–34

Arundhati Roy, *The God of Small Things*, HarperCollins, 1997

Rumi, *Whispers of the Beloved*, trans. Maryam Mafi and Azima Melita Kolin, Thorsons, 1999

Claire Sylvia, *A Change of Heart: A Memoir*, Little, Brown, 1997

Thich Nhat Hanh, *Reconciliation: Healing the Inner Child*, Parallax Press, 2010

Bessel van der Kolk, *The Body Keeps the Score: Mind, Brain and Body in the Transformation of Trauma*, Penguin, 2015

Tyler VanderWeele, 'The Power of Forgiveness', *Mind and Mood*, Harvard Health Publishing, 2021

Francis Weller, *The Wild Edge of Sorrow: Rituals of Renewal and the Sacred Work of Grief*, North Atlantic Books, 2015

William Wordsworth, 'Ode: Intimations of Immortality from Recollections of Early Childhood', *Poems, in Two Volumes*, Longman, Hurst, Rees and Orme, 1807

Connie Zweig and Jeremiah Abrams (eds), *Meeting the Shadow: The Hidden Power of the Dark Side of Human Nature*, Jeremy P. Tarcher, 1990

Acknowledgements

Many years ago, the first chapters of this book dropped into my consciousness as I sat at a kitchen table in Battersea, London. They arrived and I immediately knew that they were destined for Hay House. Fast-forward 14 years and here we are. I am profoundly grateful for this moment and for the life and spirit of Louise Hay, who created a very special container for this work. I am honoured now to be a part of this wonderful and magical family. A very special thankyou to Michelle Pilley for being all that you are and truly seeing, nurturing and inspiring me... it means the world to me! My warmest thanks and appreciation for the incredible creativity, insight and dedication of the rest of the team at Hay House, who have helped bring this book into being behind the scenes and encouraged me every step of the way: Julie Oughton, Leanne Siu Anastasi, Jo Burgess, Katherine O'Brien and Portia Chauhan, you're all amazing!

My deepest heartfelt thanks to my editor, Lizzie Henry, for your kindness, tuning in to the vision of this book and bringing your very special Libran magic to its pages. Kate Adams for meeting me at the beginning and at the end – I am so grateful for your insight and words of wisdom! Deepest appreciation and thanks to Lizzie Clark for your beautiful illustrations.

This book wouldn't have been possible without my incredible literary agent, Valeria Huerta. Thank you, Valeria, for having the unwavering passion and belief to help manifest the vision of this book and bring this work to the world.

It also wouldn't have been possible without the amazing support and patience of my partner and son. Mark Deverell, your consistent encouragement and love helped keep the 'show on the road'. Thank you so much for all that you are. I love you. And my only son, Malakai, my Taurus boy; you are the most precious and beautiful teacher. Thank you for choosing me to be your mother in this lifetime. Words can't describe how much I love you.

Remembering my beloved cousin Stephen Roachford, thank you for being my rock in this lifetime. I can feel your love, I know you are sharing this moment with me. My father for the gentleness and the laughter, Andrew Roachford for the music and sharing many dreams under a full moon, Uncle Grahame for your cheerleading, my wonderful friends who have been like family to me – Jessica, Sadie, Charlotte, Muna, Caroline, Vici, Sophie, Milly, Laura, Pens, Melodicium, I love you so much. A special shoutout to Meena Khera and Jean Paul Martinez, so blessed to have met you again in this lifetime. Meena, you're the best.

I am deeply grateful to the community and companionship of the True Essence students and practitioners for their dedication to this path of service, alchemy and the work of Love. Such a privilege to laugh, weep, eat, dance, sing and grow with you all! Mandy, Willy, Michele, Kit, Yanou, Annisa, Kate, Katherine, Tringa, Abby and all the other Mystery Schoolers – you are an inspiration!

Thank you so much Deepak Chopra, Charlotte Tilbury, Fearne Cotton, Sonia Choquette, Maude Hirst, Gaille MacKinnon and Anita Moorjani for your deep kindness and support.

I dedicate this book to every person who has contributed to *Manifest Your True Essence*, opening their hearts and sharing their stories in these pages.

I also dedicate it to every person who's ever stepped into a 1:1 session, retreat or workshop with me over the years, leaning in to trust and possibility in a new way. Thank you so much for following your heart. The True Essence process exists as a testament to your courage.

I dedicate this book to the Angels, thank you for showing up and guiding my life.

To the Ancestors, thank you sharing your wisdom with me.

And to the Divine Feminine for the path.

I dedicate this book to my mother. I love you.

Lastly, I thank God, the creator of all things, for this journey, for the power of love, for our humanity and the spirit of divinity that exists within each of us and can guide us home even in our darkest moments.

About the Author

Estelle Bingham has been supporting others to find more love, purpose and connection in their lives for over 20 years. Described as 'The Heart Whisperer', she is a fourth-generation psychic and has been meditating since she was six years old. After learning Transcendental Meditation, the journey of the Soul became an integral part of her life. She is committed to helping others heal, express their truth and embrace and embody their true joy and potential.

In her twenties, Estelle followed one of her dreams to become a journalist and TV and radio presenter, working for media organizations including the BBC, ITV and the Discovery Channel. But the universe had another plan in store...

Today, Estelle works privately on a one-to-one basis with clients in person and online in the UK and internationally. She has also been holding Sacred Full Moon circles for over 20 years, which are now held online and have brought together a rich tapestry of people from all over the world.

Estelle has been working with Body & Soul Charity for eight years, where she has been inspiring and motivating young people from adverse backgrounds to heal and dare to dream. She also leads love retreats, which offer a sacred shamanic space to facilitate long-lasting healing, transformation and manifestation.

Through her work and practice, Estelle has developed the Angelic Shamanic healing modality, which she teaches as a one-year practitioner training course.

www.estellebingham.com

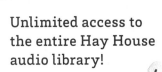

We hope you enjoyed this Hay House book. If you'd like to receive our online catalog featuring additional information on Hay House books and products, or if you'd like to find out more about the Hay Foundation, please contact:

Hay House LLC, P.O. Box 5100, Carlsbad, CA 92018-5100
(760) 431-7695 or (800) 654-5126
www.hayhouse.com® • www.hayfoundation.org

Published in Australia by:
Hay House Australia Publishing Pty Ltd
18/36 Ralph St., Alexandria NSW 2015
Phone: +61 (02) 9669 4299
www.hayhouse.com.au

Published in the United Kingdom by:
Hay House UK Ltd
1st Floor, Crawford Corner,
91–93 Baker Street, London W1U 6QQ
Phone: +44 (0)20 3927 7290
www.hayhouse.co.uk

Published in India by:
Hay House Publishers (India) Pvt Ltd
Muskaan Complex, Plot No. 3,
B-2, Vasant Kunj, New Delhi 110 070
Phone: +91 11 41761620
www.hayhouse.co.in

Let Your Soul Grow

Experience life-changing transformation—one video at a time—with guidance from the world's leading experts.

www.healyourlifeplus.com